# On
# Giants'
# Shoulders

**AMBASSADOR**

BELFAST, NORTHERN IRELAND
GREENVILLE, USA

PATRICK McELLIGOTT

To Joy, Ruth and Ann
whose courage and co-operation have
made our long-term service
in Japan possible

First edition published privately 1991
Second edition, with additional material 1994
This edition 2002

ISBN    184030 122 8

British Library' Cataloguing-in-Publication Data A catalogue record
for this book is available from the British Library

Unless otherwise stated Scripture quotations in this publication are
from the Authorised Version (Crown copyright), or The Holy Bible,
New International Version, Copyright © 1973, 1978, International
Bible Society.

*Ambassador Publications*
a division of
Ambassador Productions Ltd.
Providence House
Ardenlee Street,
Belfast,
BT6 8QJ
Northern Ireland
www.ambassador-productions.com

Emerald House
427 Wade Hampton Blvd.
Greenville
SC 29609, USA
www.emeraldhouse.com

# Contents

*As the go-betweens at a Japanese wedding.*

# Foreword to the original edition

The original purpose of this testimony was to leave a record for our children so that they would understand why they were born and brought up in the land of Japan, and why their parents made the decisions that they did, even though they resulted in a life style far from ordinary.

It was originally meant to be a personal document rather than a public one, but as I progressed with the manuscript it became obvious that it is as much your testimony as it is ours. We therefore decided to print it and share it with you, our friends and prayer partners. It comes to you with all our thanks.

We trust it will be a blessing and an encouragement to you.

Yours sincerely in Christ,

Patrick and Sarah McElligott
Kyoto, Japan
June 1991.

*Patrick (carrying his little sister) just after they moved into the council flat in Deptford 1950.*

Chapter One

# EARLY YEARS

My newfound friend did not arrive but I continued to wait, I had nothing else to do. I looked around at my new surroundings. I felt glad that we at last had a place to call home. In front of me stood a typical pre-war block of council flats, five storeys of red-brown brick with identical windows evenly spaced on every floor, capped with a sloping brown-tiled roof. The curtains at every window added a welcome splash of colour, for most of them were yet undrawn. It was nine o'clock on a Sunday morning and many people were still in bed. Nothing stirred.

Behind me stood the block of council flats into which we had recently moved. It was not quite as high as the block before me and was easily identified as a later design by the rounded balconies and the flat roof. It had been built to replace the ruins of a previous block which had been hit by a bomb during the war. The bomb had been aimed at the elevated railway line, which carried trains on their journey from the centre of London to the suburbs in the southeast. The railway line passed within fifty feet of the council flats, where it was elevated as high as the second storey by a series of dirty brick arches which were used as stables and workshops by rag-and-bone men, for which Deptford was well known. Off to my left, at the far end of the asphalt yard which stretched before the block of flats I now called home, stood yet another tall block of pre-war council flats.

Only to my immediate right was there any relief from the uniform monotony of council buildings, for across the narrow cobbled road there stood an asphalt works. Worked in to the wrought-iron gates of the asphalt works were the unlikely words, 'Val de Travers', the name of the firm. Through the gates could be seen a cobbled roadway which led down to the local canal. Being Sunday the factory was closed but the not unpleasant smell of the tar, used for making asphalt hung in the air. I breathed it in deeply for local wisdom considered it to be a healthy odour.

The sun shone and although I was disappointed that my friend had not turned up I was not unhappy. How could I be? At last we had a 'home'. I was eleven years old. We had moved to Deptford, southeast London, just a few weeks before. There were nine of us: my parents, my three brothers, my two sisters, an old lady who lived with us, and myself. It was partly because we were such a large family that we had lived 'on the welfare' for years.

We originally lived in Peckham, a London borough just west of Deptford. I was born there two months before the commencement of the Second World War. My memories of life in Peckham are scant but I can recall the huge bonfire in the road to celebrate the end of the war, and the red-bricked 'water tank' built in our road during the war as a reservoir to aid the fire brigade in its efforts to put out fires during the air raids, and playing endless games of football in the street with an old tin can, or at best with a tennis ball upon which there remained not one scrap of 'fur'. In fact, it was not until much later that I realised that tennis balls were white and furry, not black and smooth.

The joy and general optimism which pervaded society after the war did not last long in our household. Father injured himself at work and was demoted from the promising occupation of lift-engineer to that of general electrician with the Ministry of Works. His wages were reduced and times began to get hard for us. So hard that, unbeknown to father, mother stopped paying the rent. We lived in the basement of a terraced house. We used the first-floor rooms as bedrooms. The landlady lived upstairs. She was a nice enough old lady but after months of nonpayment of the rent, accompanied by threats from her to have us evicted, she did just that. She called the bailiffs and we were put out of the house. With a growing family and father in a poorly-paid job, my parents could not cope financially. Father did not know that we were so far behind with the rent. The whole episode was a great shock to him, a shock from which I believe he never truly recovered. He tended to be remote from all of us afterwards. Consequently, none of us children ever really got to know him well. For years after the war housing was scarce in London. Bomb damage had been extensive. Large, poor, working-class families were particularly difficult to house. Having nowhere else to go, we were cast on the benevolence of the welfare state. Thus began our life 'on the welfare'.

For the next few years we were moved from one 'reception centre' to another. A reception centre was a government-run, temporary abode for homeless families. In our experience no two were alike. At one time we lived in a large musty-smelling house just off Sloane Square in the fashionable borough of Chelsea. The address was impressive: Cadogan Gardens. The house had dark wood-panelled walls and bare, creaky, wooden staircases. It was dimly lit. Even in the daytime it seemed to me that an air of foreboding pervaded it. I was frightened of the staircases, especially at night. I always ran up or down them to our room or to the front door.

We were given one room for the whole family. It was a large room with a very high ceiling. Father divided the room by placing a large blanket over a rope, which he strung from wall to wall. We ate, played and slept in the one room. We later lived in a completely different kind of reception centre in Islington, north London. It was more like a hospital. There were various dormitories and rooms. Mother and her two baby daughters lived in a dormitory with other mothers and their young children. Father and his four sons lived in a completely separate dormitory for men and boys. I can still recall the white tiled walls of the men's dormitory and the way we used to look forward to Sunday afternoons when we could visit mother. Our greatest treat was to all go to the local park together.

It was a hard life. It is a blessing to me that my memories of it are so scant. Between the age of five and eleven years I went to five different primary schools. I have just one really vivid memory of primary school: my first confessional. Being Roman Catholics we were sent to Roman Catholic schools, where we were taught the catechism and taken regularly to mass. At school I was prepared for my first confession when I was nine years old. After the preparation I went with my classmates to the local Catholic church where we lined up outside the confessional box. When my turn came I went in and spoke to the priest as I had been instructed. I could not see the priest's face as it was hidden behind a fine mesh screen and there was no light in the confessional box. However, I heard his voice clearly, it was kind and gentle. He told me to say a number of 'Hail Mary' prayers and a number of 'Our Father' prayers. I stepped out of the tiny cubicle and knelt in the pews with the other children. It was then that one of the nuns who taught us at school noticed that I did not have a rosary. When we arrived back at the school she called me to her office and presented me with a rosary of white and brown beads on a fine silver chain from which hung a small wooden crucifix edged with silver. It had a little case of its own. I was thrilled to receive it. I treasured it for years.

My only other clear memory of primary schools is that of large asphalt playgrounds where we played football every evening after school until it became so dark we could no longer see the ball.

After years of this nomadic existence, in 1950 our dreams came true. We were given a 'home of our own'. We were granted a large, new council flat in Deptford. It was a four-bedroomed flat on the top floor. From the back windows we looked down on the elevated railway line and the brick arches that carried it. We were very excited. When we all went to see it for the first time we wanted to move in there and then. In addition to the four bedrooms it had a kitchen, a living room and a bathroom. With very little furniture we moved in. I can recall clearly the thrill of sleeping in 'my bedroom' for what seemed the first time in my life, even though I did share it with my older brother, and initially it had only mattresses on the floor.

Thus we came to live in Deptford where, at St. Joseph's, the local Roman Catholic primary school, I had made a new friend. It was for this friend that I waited in the courtyard amidst the dull silence of sleepy inactivity which prevailed most Sunday mornings in the council flats.

Into the entrance at the far end of the courtyard came a man on a bicycle. Though well over a hundred yards away, I noticed him immediately for nothing else moved. He looked different from anybody I had ever seen in the flats before. To me he appeared strangely dressed. He wore a dark blue suit, black shiny shoes, a white shirt, a black tie, and on his head was perched a wedge-shaped, navy-blue hat with two little black ribbons at the back.

He had an official air about him. I immediately assumed he was some kind of policeman. I stood my ground as nearer and nearer he came. I tried to avoid looking at him but was aware that he had an interest in me. I hoped he would just cycle past but, to my dismay, he stopped his bicycle immediately in front of me. He got off and walked towards me. I was filled with a sense of apprehension.

"What are you doing sonny?" he asked in a posh sort of voice. By this time I was sure he was a policeman.

"Nuffin, mister. I ain't doing nuffin," I replied defensively.

"Oh good! Why not come with me to the Boys' Brigade Bible Class then?" he asked with a smile on his face.

He was the local Boys' Brigade captain out scouring the streets for boys who had nothing to do. I was so relieved that he wasn't a policeman that I went with him.

We walked together through the quiet streets, past the primary school and the large Roman Catholic church in the High Street, until we came to a narrow deadend street that I had not noticed before, even though I had been up and down the High Street a number of times. At the end of this narrow road stood an ancient looking mission hall, upon the wall of which hung a wooden notice board which displayed the words 'The Princess Louise Institute, a Branch of The Shaftesbury Society'. I would never have recognised it as a church. The contrast between the imposing Roman Catholic churches to which I was accustomed could hardly have been greater. Even the name of the place did not suggest a church of any kind. Inside, the contrast was stark. I was led into a small side room. It had plain walls and a bare wooden floor. An old piano stood in one corner. There was not a statue, an altar, a candlestick, not even a candle to be seen anywhere! I cannot recall the content of that first Boys' Brigade Bible Class, but I shall never forget the little group of boys I met there. No boy could wish to find better friends than those boys were to become to me. There were about a dozen boys in the room. They welcomed me warmly. Some were considerably older than I was but it made no difference, for they also made me feel at ease.

From the moment I stepped into that little room the pattern of my life in Deptford changed completely. I soon discovered that the Boys' Brigade had a football team, did sports training and gymnastics, played cricket and went swimming together. They also had a brass band and a weekly youth club with table tennis and snooker. Four, sometimes five nights a week I would be with the other boys at the mission hall. The Friday night youth club and the Saturday afternoon football match became the highlights of my weekend. Sunday morning also became busier for me. After the nine o'clock mass at the Roman Catholic church I ran up the High Street to be at the Bible Class before it started at ten.

It was not without a sense of guilt that I hurried from the beautifully-decorated Catholic church to the old mission hall, for we were taught at school that we should not attend Protestant places of worship. But Bible Class was compulsory and I was rarely absent. To my shame I remember little of what I was taught at the Bible Class. All I can recall are the stories of St. Paul and his travels. Blinded one week, shipwrecked the next, bitten by snakes, put in prison, beaten and whipped, to a twelve-year-old they were thrilling stories, but it never occurred to me to think why Paul endured all these things! I thought he was some kind of madman, and in any case I usually had one eye on the clock!

So glad was I to have found this little group of boys who became my friends, that I told my best friend at school about the mission hall, the football team and the other activities. He, too, began to attend but, as a Roman Catholic, he felt very guilty about the Bible Class and stopped coming. The local priest visited our house from time to time. My mother was embarrassed about my attendance at the mission hall, but nothing would have stopped me going there. I had found what I had craved for during our 'nomadic' years 'on the welfare'. I had found real friends.

I did not realise it at the time but some of the older boys were followers of Christ. They 'loved me for His sake'. Even though my school friend stopped coming to the mission hall for a while, he began to attend again. Like me, he later became a follower of Christ, and to this day is a member of the Shaftesbury Christian Centre, the present name for the Princess Louise Institute.

Though Roman Catholics my parents were glad to see me off the streets, even though I spent so much time at the mission hall. Deptford was a rough place. Roaming the streets could be dangerous for a young teenager.

Economic necessity demanded that both my mother and my father worked at fulltime jobs. Bringing up six young children under such circumstances was not an easy task. Both mother and father left the house before we set out for school. Neither were home when we returned.

The economic life of Deptford had for centuries been sustained by its proximity to the River Thames. Traditionally it was a place where oceangoing sailing ships were repaired and refitted and where ships' stores were replenished. Deptford has always been a 'poor relation' to the more fashionable, famous and royal borough of Greenwich just along the Thames, where to this day the Naval Hospital still stands by the riverside, and where the National Maritime Museum is housed in a once royal residence surrounded by Greenwich Park, which was royal park land.

Deptford has always been 'working class'. Even the mission hall which was to become my 'spiritual home' had started its ministry in the mid-nineteenth century as a Ragged School for poor children.

In the 1950s Deptford was the home of dockers, factory workers and labourers. It was also a centre of the rag-and-bone trade. Even in the 1960s the 'totters' horse and cart, laden down with old bedsteads, bundles of rags and other assorted junk, was a common sight. The distinctive high-pitched calls of the rag-and-bone men for 'lumber' often pierced the air.

The social life of Deptford was centred almost entirely in the local pubs. In Deptford High Street alone, a street of just a few hundred yards, there were at least ten pubs. Their exotic names fascinated me as a boy. The Harp of Erin, The Noah's Ark, The Brown Bear and The Globe. Other local pubs reflected in their names the maritime history of Deptford, The Hoy Inn, The Admiral Benbow and The Lord Nelson. The signboards outside these pubs appeared to me to be works of art. My dad's favourite pub was The Robin Hood, though I was never sure why a pub in Deptford had such a name! It stood just a few yards from the entrance to the block of flats in which we lived. Many a time I waited outside its doors on a Saturday night for a bottle of lemonade. On Sunday afternoons I sometimes went there to call him home for Sunday lunch.

Deptford also boasted the biggest 'dosshouse' in southeast London, a huge red-bricked building which provided cheap lodgings for the many 'down and outs' that Deptford seemed to attract. The white tiled interior walls reminded me of the reception centre in Islington. I did not like the place. It was called Charrington House. Its presence assured Deptford of more than its fair share of tramps and alcoholics who wiled away their time sitting in public places, church porches and park benches clutching their bottles of beer or cheap wine. Some even resorted to drinking methylated spirits. At night the poorest could be found huddled up in shop entrances sleeping on newspapers to keep out the cold. As a boy I felt sorry for them but accepted them as a fact of life. They never seemed to me to cause much trouble. Some of them were even cheerful and friendly. They were all part of life in Deptford.

Mother worked at the local Peak Freans biscuit factory at a conveyor belt, sorting biscuits. She left home at about 7.30am and returned about 6.30pm. On her return she would immediately start to prepare something for father to eat for his supper. We children had usually eaten by the time mother arrived home. We all looked forward to Friday nights when mother would bring home a large bag of broken biscuits. She carefully shared them out amongst us, for if the cream or chocolate biscuits were not divided equally a fight would result! After we moved from Peckham father remained a Ministry of Works electrician for the rest of his life. He left the house earlier than mother in the mornings, but was normally home by six in the evening. When he bought a newspaper it was usually the communist Daily Worker: He had stopped going to church many years previously, and would not talk about church at all.

Money was always a problem, it normally ran out by Wednesday each week! It was a constant struggle to find fares to work and dinner money for Thursdays, when dad got paid again. Apart from the food we ate, much of what mother purchased was on credit. The 'tallyman' was our most regular caller. As young children we knew why such purchasing was known as 'on the never never'. The bills never seemed to be paid completely. Before one purchase was completed another had been made. Sometimes both mother and father would arrange to be out of the house rather than be in when the 'tallyman' called for more money.

It was not so much that we lived beyond our means. Rather that mother and father had never acquired the habit of managing their finances. Financial stress was part of life.

Yet ours was not an unhappy home. Like most poorer working-class Deptford families, ours too was buoyed by a constant sense of optimism. Humour was never far from the surface, we were no strangers to laughter. Things were always going to 'take a turn for the better', something was always 'going to turn up', and we constantly looked forward to the day when 'our ship would come in'!

This attitude was typified by the deathly hush father always commanded at five o'clock every Saturday afternoon when the football results were broadcast on the radio and he checked his football coupon. We held our breath as one result followed another and listened to father's little groans of disappointment. To my knowledge he hardly ever won a penny, but disappointment was soon forgotten, next week was always going to be better!

Life was also punctuated by the occasional 'family knees up'. Aunts, uncles and family friends would gather at our flat on a Saturday night to drink, dance and sing before dropping off to sleep in odd corners all over the flat. As we got older we children also joined in the revelry.

After one such party I woke up to find myself on the living room table where I had spent the night with a friend. We had slept there for hours, covered with tea towels. To this day I have no idea how we got there. It remains a mystery to me how we stayed there half the night without falling off!

Money was spent on such 'good times' with a gay abandon that excluded any thought for the fact that no one would have any money for fares or dinners by Wednesday night.

Our constant weekly financial crisis affected our lives in many ways. Rows about money were frequent. They usually resulted in mother weeping and father going off to the pub or sitting sulking in his armchair while we children instinctively kept a low profile, especially us boys, for although my father would never strike mother or his daughters there were times when he lost his temper with us boys. Mother and father were constantly tired. With them both working at fulltime jobs we grew up learning to fend for ourselves.

It was mainly because of this that an elderly lady came to live with us. I was never sure what connection she had with our family. She was certainly not related to us in any way. She was a frail little spinster with long grey hair always tied up in a huge bun held in place with numerous hairpins. She wore round, metal-rimmed spectacles. She was quiet and timid. Her name was Lilian but with typical 'cockney' wit we chose a most inappropriate name for this elderly lady. We called her Lulu. It was a mystery to me why she stayed with us, for every now and again she would take a trip out to the suburbs of southeast London to meet her relatives who were quite well off.

Her life with us was one of constant misery. Father never agreed to her coming, would never speak to her unless it was to growl a complaint, would not touch a thing she cooked, and would not allow her into the living room if he was there. He constantly insisted that she was 'moulting all over the place'.

She spent most of her time in her room, one of the four precious bedrooms. Having her with us meant that the four youngest children had to share one room. None of us children took any notice of her whatsoever. We cheeked her, disobeyed her, swore at her, and systematically stole from her meagre 'old age pension'. There was no place she could hide her little store of money that we could not find. With six children in the house, with a father who turned a deaf ear to her appeals to find the culprit, there was no solution to her problem. The culprit was never found because by and large all us boys were culprits. Many times it was simply a case of who would find the money first. She was often in tears.

Having her in the flat was probably a matter of mutual convenience. She, it seems, had nowhere else to go and was given a room free of charge. She was paid no wages and 'looked after' us children while mum and dad both worked. When the younger children reached the stage where they could look after themselves she left and went into an old people's institution. Looking back I am ashamed that we made her life such a miserable one.

Indoors during the cold winter months we spent each evening in the living room where the only fire was lit. We either listened to the radio, or in later years watched the television. Dad would doze off in his armchair, while mum would sit knitting or darning while she drank from her mug of tea. Very rarely did anyone ever read a book or do any homework. There were no musical instruments in the house although at one time some friends and I tried to form our own jazz band. Practice had to be suspended at our house for the sake of the neighbours. During the warm, lighter, summer evenings, if I were not at the mission hall I would play football or cricket in the courtyard in front of the flats or roam the streets until it became dark. It was there that I learned to smoke and first tasted drink.

The streets of Deptford were sometimes places of violence, especially on Saturday nights after the pubs had closed. Fighting outside the pubs was not uncommon. Shouts of "Fight! Fight!", or the more colloquial "Bundle!", always attracted a crowd of onlookers who would urge the contestants on.

One night on my way home from the mission hall I answered the cry of "Bundle!" only to find that one of the combatants was my elder brother. It was a violent and bloody brawl outside a pub. My brother later arrived home with a black eye and a swollen mouth, but his dignity was intact. He had proved himself and I was not ashamed of him.

At another time, late one Saturday night, there was a fight in the courtyard in front of our flats. To my surprise father was one of the contestants! He came home none the worse for wear.

Returning home late one dark night from the local cinema I was held up at knife point by a small gang of older boys who demanded all I possessed. Terrified, I ran home. I had learned to be wiser at the cost of two shillings and a penknife.

The Shaftesbury mission hall and the friends I made there became the centre of my life. The mission hall had a stabilising influence upon my teenage years, but it did not deliver me from the effects of the constant economic battle that we had as a family, or from the temptations that life in Deptford presented me with.

Mother could never find sufficient money to keep us properly clothed for school. Indeed, we had little respect for our clothing and wore out shoes, shirts and trousers with alarming speed. I remember cutting up cornflake packets to save my socks from wearing out through the holes in my shoes. I even experimented with tin inner soles cut from a large cocoa tin, but when it rained the tin rusted! Deptford, being a centre for the rag-and-bone trade, had no shortage of secondhand clothing stalls at the local market but these too had to be paid for, and the wily stall-holders were quick to spot the potential shoplifter. The constant economic battle eventually led to mother's downfall. She loved us children very much. She hated to see us so poorly dressed. A couple of years after we moved to Deptford, shortly after my thirteenth birthday, I went with mother one Saturday afternoon to help with the shopping. I did this quite often when there was no football match to be played. We went on the bus to the next borough, Lewisham, where there were much bigger department stores than any in Deptford. In the British Home Stores mother began to fill the large bag she was carrying with articles of children's clothing. She did not pay for them. Outside the store two smartly dressed men apprehended us and led us back into the store. We were escorted through a side door which led upstairs to a small office. We had been arrested for shoplifting. Mother began to cry and insisted she had simply forgotten to pay for the goods. The police arrived and began to ask routine questions. The store detectives insisted upon charging both of us, declaring to the police that we were working as a team. Mother confessed to her own shoplifting signed a statement and then proceeded to proclaim my innocence. We went home on the bus in tears.

A few days later mother was summoned to appear at the local magistrates' court. To our utter dismay she was sentenced to serve six months in Holloway Women's Prison. The judge insisted on a prison sentence because, even though mother was a first-time offender, her crime was serious. She was supposedly teaching a minor how to steal. I was not charged with anything.

We meekly accepted the sentence, not knowing that such a sentence for a first-time offence could have been appealed against.

So mother went to prison. We told everyone that she had simply 'gone away for a few months'. Most people understood what was meant. The six months passed slowly, but mother was eventually released. It never seemed strange to me at the time that I was the only one to meet her at the gates of Holloway Prison when she came out.

Life soon got back to normal. We loved our mother nonetheless for her experience. I personally was more convinced of her love for us than ever. With no job to go back to at the biscuit factory, mother started a 'new' job at the Crosse & Blackwell canned goods factory in Bermondsey. There she worked as a 'bean sorter'. She had simply exchanged one conveyor belt for another.

Mother loved her children. She worked hard to keep us clothed and fed but it was a constant struggle. Economic necessity influenced many important family decisions. By some means or other I passed my eleven-plus examinations at St. Joseph's primary school in the High Street. The headmaster informed my parents that I should go for an interview at the nearest Roman Catholic grammar school in nearby Blackheath. Having heard this I walked up the steep hill that leads from Deptford to the more fashionable borough of Blackheath to spy out the grammar school. I discovered that the children wore gold braided blazers, grey flannel trousers and black shiny shoes.

I never went for the interview. Mum felt she could not afford to keep me in such a uniform  not knowing that she could probably obtain a grant to cover such costs. In any case, it was altogether too 'posh'.

All in the family agreed that I would not be happy there. They were undoubtedly right.

The next closest Roman Catholic secondary school was in Stepney in the 'east end', right in the heart of cockney London. For the next four years I commuted by tube train, under the Thames, to St. Bernard's Central School. St Bernard's was full of children who came mainly from the east end of London. Most of them were 'our kind of people'. Even though I wore short trousers for longer than almost all the other boys, put margarine on my hair to make it shine, filled the holes in my shoes with cornflake boxes and went to school on a breakfast of bread and dripping I was not out of place. I was happy there.

After five years at St Bernard's I sat eight O level exams and passed four, including Maths and English. How I achieved that much was to me quite remarkable, for I was never a zealous student. I rarely did much homework at home, but rushed to school early in the mornings to do it at the school

It was perhaps due more to the fact that I discovered the joys of reading just after my thirteenth birthday that I was able to pass four O level exams. It happened by accident. One of my younger sisters was ill and confined to bed. I was sent to the local library to get books to help keep her occupied. When I took the books I had chosen to the librarian to have them stamped I was told I could choose one more. I decided to get one for myself.

I searched among the rows of books for something that interested me until I noticed on the spine of a book in the adventure section a picture of an aircraft being shot down in flames. I added the book to the pile and took it home. In bed that night I began to read it. It was so interesting I could not put it down.

With a torch under the blankets I continued to read until I had finished it. The following day I went back to the library to see if they had any more books like the one I had read. The librarian took me to a shelf and pointed to a whole row of them, all by the same author, all about the same adventurer. I was 'hooked' on 'Biggles'! From that day on I was invariably reading something.

Although life was hard there were also many happy times. Like most boys in similar circumstances we had to earn our own pocket money. My elder brother worked as a 'barrow boy' on a fruit stall in the High Street on Saturdays. One of my younger brothers had a part-time job in a local tailor's shop. My pocket-money activity was more conventional. I did a paper round for one hour after school each day and spent the early hours of Sunday morning trudging the quiet streets humping a heavy bag of Sunday newspapers up seemingly endless flights of council flat stairs. There were no elevators in council flats in those days. The strap of the large canvas bag cut into my shoulder, which became painful at the beginning of the round but eased as the bag got lighter. However, the joy of receiving ten shillings a week for this task will always remain with me.

For a few years I also did a baker's round on Saturday mornings, carrying the heavy wicker basket full of loaves to the top floors of the council flats where the rounds-man did not care to go. It was hard work but made enjoyable by the fact that I was allowed to drive the horse and wagon down the quieter streets, was allowed to help myself to a few cream cakes, and received a few precious shillings at the end of the round.

It was with money thus earned that I bought my first bicycle from the rag-and-bone man and saved up for the annual Boys' Brigade camp. Every year we went to Shanklin on the Isle of Wight. We used the same tents, in the same field, on the same farm, with the same friends and did the same things year after year, but we were never bored!

The school urged me to stay on in the sixth form and try for A levels, but it was out of the question. Mother, expressing the collective wisdom of the family, left the choice to me, saying, "It's up to you, son, but if you get a job you will get a wage."

Having no particular desire for two more years at school, I left St Bernard's just after my sixteenth birthday and started work as a cost and works accountant trainee at Crosse & Blackwell of Bermondsey where mother worked as a 'bean sorter'. The job involved frequent trips from the office to the factory floor where I had to time the speed of the canning machines with a stopwatch. The speed of the machines determined the level of the bonus of the women working them. Mother was very proud of me in my white 'management' coat. I usually received a cheerful welcome from mother and the six or seven other women who sat hour after hour at the conveyor belt picking out discoloured beans before they went into the cans. Often, as I approached in my long white coat, the machine minder would slightly increase the speed of the machine for a few moments so that when I timed it the result would give the women a little extra bonus payment. Often the machine speed was quickened when I was just coming to get my lunchtime sandwiches from mother!

With more money to spend I supplemented my life at the mission hall with visits to jazz clubs, all-night drinking and gambling parties, and a more positive participation in the family 'knees ups'. A crate of beer, bottles of spirits, cigars, a record player and a pack of cards would often occupy us all through Saturday night. We would turn up at the Boys' Brigade Bible Class bleary eyed at ten o'clock Sunday morning. After Bible Class we would walk over Blackheath, down through Greenwich Park, pop into a pub for a quick pre-dinner pint and then go to our respective homes.

During this time I occasionally attended the Sunday evening gospel service at the mission hall, and sat through all the Billy Graham relay meetings. Every year, at the Boys' Brigade summer camp, we had gospel messages and Bible studies night after night.

As far as I can remember, not once during these years did I ever seriously consider the claims of Christ on my life. I still attended mass at the Roman Catholic church on rare occasions.

*Boys' Brigade Football Team, Patrick is fourth from the right*

Chapter Two

# A CHANGED LIFE

It was a typical Saturday. It began with no indication whatever of how dramatically it would end. In the morning I worked overtime at Crosse & Blackwell. I enjoyed this for the extra pocket money it produced. In the afternoon I waited at the top of Deptford High Street for the distinctive red and green Crosse & Blackwell's lorry which carried the work's football team out to the suburbs for the weekly match. As usual it was late, but it eventually arrived and stopped at the curb where I stood.

The football team were in the back of the covered lorry in various stages of undress. Because they were late everyone was getting ready to go straight from the lorry on to the football pitch. As the back door of the lorry was opened to let me in, the half-dressed football team was exposed to the gaze of the amused shoppers who thronged the High Street on Saturday afternoons. Hoots of laughter and ribald comments filled the air as I was swiftly hauled up into the lorry which soon sped on its way. We lost 4-1 that afternoon to Charringtons, the brewers. I was not unduly concerned at losing, for that night I was going to a party.

At the mission hall I had learned how to play table tennis. I had progressed sufficiently enough to be included in the team that represented the mission hall in a local league. The captain of our team, a young man my own age named John, had invited me to his girl friend's birthday party at her home in Eltham, which was a thirty-minute bus ride from Deptford. I had accepted the invitation without hesitation. The word 'party' has a happy ring to it. However, when I got there I felt very disappointed. Everyone drank orange juice and played what seemed to me to be childish games. It was not my idea of a party at all!

I sat in the corner reading the evening newspaper. I felt I had been tricked into being there. I was reluctant to join in the games but eventually began to do so. Then just after ten o'clock, to my surprise, the party was declared over. People started to go home.

As I prepared to take my leave my friend John asked me to help him carry a record player and some records to his home. John, too, lived in the council flats in Deptford not far from my home, so I agreed to help him.

We arrived at his parents' flat about eleven o'clock. He invited me in for a cup of coffee. I readily accepted his invitation and entered the flat. All was quiet. His parents had either gone to bed or were not at home. The two of us sat in the kitchen talking and drinking coffee. We talked about table tennis, football, cricket and sports in general. Midnight passed yet still we sat in the quiet kitchen. One o'clock came and went, yet we talked on into the night.

Close to two o'clock John stopped talking about sports, produced a Bible and began to talk to me about Jesus Christ. Instinctively I felt that I had been tricked again! I knew quite well that he could have managed to carry the records and record player by himself. I felt he had just used them as an excuse to get me alone in his kitchen so that he could talk to me about Christ. I resented this and began to argue with him. I purposefully disagreed with everything he said. I became quite irritated and tried to remember the things I had been taught at school. I felt I knew more about God than John.

It did not seem to matter how irritated I became. John never lost his temper. He met all my arguments quietly and consistently with Bible verses prefixed with words like, "Ah! Yes Pat, but God says ...", "But Pat, God's Word says ...". From two o'clock till three o'clock we talked and discussed, but I was determined not to be persuaded.

Around three o'clock John closed his Bible and put it to one side. I immediately thought I had won the day! I was ready to go home.

His Bible set to one side, John said, "Pat, I want you to listen to an imaginary story and then give me your opinion about it."
I agreed to listen.
John went on, "Imagine two young men, good friends for many years, walking along a busy road. One of them decides to go to a shop on the other side of the road. He steps off the pavement into the road. As he is crossing the road a lorry comes racing towards him. He is unaware of his great danger. His friend still on the pavement realises the situation, runs into the road and pushes him from the path of the onrushing lorry. In doing so he is himself struck by the lorry and killed.
"Pat, what would you do if you were the young man who had been pushed from the path of the lorry and was safe?"
I did not answer immediately but asked for a few moments to think. I thought to myself "What is a good moral and respectable answer to this question?" I did not think about what I would actually do. Rather, I searched for a clever answer. After a few minutes thought I decided what my answer would be.
I replied, "John, I would go to my dead friend's parents. I would thank them for their son and his friendship. I would thank them that their son gave his life saving mine. I would tell them that I would do anything I could to make up for his death. I would try to be a son to them. I would do whatever they asked me to do."
John was delighted with my answer. He promptly reached out for his Bible again, and opened it at these words:
*"For when we were yet without strength, in due time Christ died for the ungodly. For scarcely for a righteous man will one die: yet peradventure for a good man some would even dare to die. But God commendeth His love toward us, in that, while we were yet sinners Christ died for us."* (Romans 5: 68).
John then asked me if I had ever said 'Thank you' to my heavenly Father for sending His Son Jesus to die in my stead. I replied that I had not.
Through his simple illustration I became aware of a profound yet simple truth. God loved me. It was suddenly so personal, so individual. John explained to me that even if I were the only sinner on earth, the

only person who needed a Saviour, Jesus would still have come and died for me! God loved me that much! I began to realise that I was somehow important to God. I knew that I could be different.

I was now eager to listen. All my life I had heard that God was love. I had often felt that, because God was in heaven, somehow everything would be all right one day. But this was different, John began to show me from the Bible that I needed to pray, to confess my sinfulness, thank my heavenly Father for sending Jesus Christ to be my Saviour and receive the gift of a clean heart. John assured me from the Scriptures that Jesus would come and dwell in my heart. Around four o'clock in the morning John read to me these wonderful words, *"If we confess our sins, he is faithful and just to forgive us our sins, and to cleanse us from all unrighteousness.* (1 John 1:9).

"Do you want to ask Jesus Christ into your heart as Saviour?" John asked

"Yes," was my instant reply.

"Well, then," said John. "Do it now!"

With all my heart I wanted to pray, but I could not. John urged me to kneel on the floor and pray, but something held me back, I was nervous, embarrassed, I did not have courage to do it. It was a strange feeling. It was like attempting to dive from a high board for the first time. I wanted to do it, but I held back. It was as if I was on the very edge of the board but with my big toes stuck fast!

John was a wise friend. He knew my predicament "I'll help you," he said "Let's kneel together."

So saying, he put his hand on my shoulder and we knelt together on the kitchen floor. It was perfectly silent. John, his hand still on my shoulder, whispered to me to pray. I began to pray. What a childish prayer it seemed to me as I stumbled through the words, "Father, I am sorry I have never said 'Thank you' to you for sending Jesus to be my Saviour. Thank you for sending Him. Thank you that He died for me. I ask you to cleanse my heart from sin. I now ask Jesus to come into my heart and live there. Amen."

Then John prayed. We rose from the floor and sat on our chairs. I have never been the same since then. The love of God had come into my heart and life. John shared a few more verses from the Bible with me about confessing Christ to others, after which I prepared to leave for home.

Just as I was about to go John asked me to make him a promise. I agreed to do so. I asked what it was. He then asked me to promise him that I would tell the first person I met next day what had happened to me. I made my promise to him and stepped out into the rain.

The rain was drizzling down. It was dark and gloomy. The street lamps were out. I walked quickly home, singing in my heart the choruses I had learned at the Boys' Brigade Bible Class. I now knew what they meant. I arrived home, let myself in and went straight to bed.

I slept for a few hours, rose early and went out into the kitchen to make some tea. Mother was already up and working there. When I saw her I remembered my promise to John.

"Mum, I am sorry I was out so late last night," I spluttered out. She was surprised because we did not usually apologise for such things. "Mum, last night something wonderful happened to me," I continued. Mum's eyes brightened. "What was it, son? What was it?" she asked eagerly, thinking perhaps I'd won at the bingo or something.

"Last night, Mum, I gave my heart to Jesus Christ. I became a real Christian."

Mother did not know what to say. I had taken her completely by surprise. In her perplexity she responded, "Don't worry son, it'll only be a nine-day wonder!"

The change in my life was dramatic. The mission hall was now not only at the centre of my social life, it was also my spiritual home. I never set foot in the Roman Catholic church for the next twenty-eight years. I stopped smoking, drinking and gambling. Some of my friends also came to Christ.

The change in me was most noticeable at home. My older brother simply did not know what to think of me each night as I knelt by my bed to pray and read my Bible. He soon learned just to ignore me.

Poor Lulu stood nonplussed, literally unable to speak when I presented her with a sum of money which I thought would repay her for all I had stolen from her pension over the years. Bewildered, she began to cry. Nothing like this had ever happened to her before in our home.

I became an avid reader of Christian books. I frequently visited the Christian Literature Crusade bookshop in Ludgate Hill near St Paul's Cathedral. I fixed a little bookshelf over the end of my bed. Soon it groaned under the weight of such tomes as *Wesley's Sermons, Whitefield's Journals* and *Readings from C H Spurgeon.*

In the winter months when it was too cold to read in the bedroom, I decided to read in the living room while everyone else watched television. I determined to show my family that a Christian was free from the influence of 'Satan's silver screen', (That was what television was called by the pastor at the mission hall). I would show them that a Christian is much better employed reading a good book!

Whitefield's Journals in hand I positioned my chair in the only place I thought I would not be tempted to watch the television, right next to the television itself facing everyone else. The whole family sat in a semicircle looking at the television screen and the back of my book. They must have thought I was mad. I soon found that bursts of laughter at the antics of comedian Tony Hancock, or gasps of excitement at some sporting event, were too much for Whitefield's Journals to compete with. I often found myself craning my neck around the book to see what was happening on the screen. I quickly abandoned this form of witness. It was not popular at all.

One other attempt at 'witnessing' to my family proved even more unpopular. A small group of us newly-converted young men decided that we would use our Sunday afternoons trying to tell our respective families about Christ. Our major problem was how to do this. We were at a loss until someone came up with the idea of simply conversing loudly in front of our families about Christ and the joys of being a Christian. It was my family's turn to be 'witnessed to' but we had formidable opposition.

There was a football match on the television. The whole family wanted to watch it. There was no way we could get a hearing with a football match on the 'telly'. We sat in the corner of the room not knowing what to do. The rest of my family were getting ready to watch the match. Chairs were positioned, bags of crisps and cups of tea made ready, the television finely tuned.

To the surprise of the rest of us one of our number suggested that we pray, that we pray specifically for the television to break down. We all thought this was a most appropriate challenge to our faith and told the one who had suggested it to pray himself. He prayed that the television would break down. In a few minutes the picture on the screen deteriorated and the screen became a white fuzzy mess.

My father and elder brother, both electricians, fiddled confidently with the knobs at the back of the television set, but to no avail. The four of us sat in the corner talking loudly about our faith, while the family fumed and hurled curses at the television set. No picture could be obtained. The family abandoned television viewing for the afternoon.

After we felt we had 'witnessed' enough we decided to leave. As my friends and I headed for the front door my elder brother came with us. In my unwise zeal I told him that I knew why the television had broken down. He was very interested. I told him that one of my friends had prayed against it. I thought he would be impressed by the power of prayer.

Instead he retorted, "Which one was it? If he shows his face around here again I'll punch his nose in for 'im!" The television never went wrong again.

My newfound faith also brought me some unsought-for popularity within the family. No longer needing money for jazz clubs, drink, cigarettes or cinemas, I suddenly became 'rich'. I found my weekly wage was more than sufficient for my needs. I became the first member of our family to start to systematically save money. I opened a Post Office Savings Account, and put a set amount into it each week. I thus became the family 'banker'. If anyone needed money for fares or dinners on the days before pay day they knew they could come to me for a loan! I became, in the words of my mother, "The only sensible one among us."

My work-mates also soon noticed the difference that had taken place in my life. The language in the back of the football lorry began to show a marked change once the team had picked me up at Deptford. The men could tell that I would no longer join in the swearing and crude jokes. In the office, too, although there were many taunts of 'Holy Joe', gradually my colleagues began to respect my position and accept me as 'different'. I began to attend the Workers' Christian Fellowship which met at the Bermondsey Medical Mission, next door to the factory. It was here that I first had the opportunity to preach the gospel to the many factory workers who gathered at our annual evangelistic meetings.

*Patrick just after conversion, outside the mission hall in Deptford 1956, age 17.*

My biggest challenge at work came when the Chief Accountant rang our office and demanded that I tell any callers that he was out. I said that I was unable to do so. He demanded that I come immediately to his office to explain myself. I concluded that I might lose my job, but determined that it would be worth it rather than lie.

He confronted me with the fact that he was a very busy man and did not wish to be disturbed. I replied that I was quite willing to tell any callers that he could not be disturbed. I also insisted that I could not tell callers he was out if I knew he was in!

He asked me why. I told him it was a matter of conscience, and explained to him that I was a Christian. Somewhat taken aback by my impudence he apologised. He then told me to go back to my office and pray that the phone would not ring! A few months later he recommended me for an unscheduled twenty-percent pay rise for conscientious work.

Some eighteen months after my conversion I was called up to do national service. I passed my medical Al and decided to do three years in the Royal Air Force. Shortly after the medical I was given a joining date and told to report at Wilmslow in Cheshire for 'square-bashing'. Just after I enlisted, the government abolished national service. I was in the very last batch of young men to be called up. I thought it most unfair, but was later to look back with much thankfulness for my experiences while a serviceman.

Just before I went away to do the eight weeks' basic training, one of the older Christians at the mission hall called me aside and gave me some advice. He was a godly man. His advice was good and sound. He urged me to determine in my heart that I would witness boldly to the fact that I was a Christian. He said it would be best if I committed myself to witnessing on the very first night of billet life. He assured me that if I did not witness on the first night it would be more difficult on the second night and even more difficult on the third.

His advice was good but it had the wrong effect upon me. Instead of casting myself on the Lord and trusting Him for strength to witness, I told myself that no one was going to stop me witnessing. I would show them what I stood for! Rather than seeking power from the Lord, my attitude was more like, 'Leave it to me, Lord; I won't let you down!'

My first night in the billet was one to be remembered. No one wanted to be there. Everyone declared that life was very unfair because they had been called up in the very last batch to do national service. Some just grumbled and cursed their luck, whilst others played cards, told jokes, sang songs and generally larked about. In the middle of all this I decided to go to bed. It was then that I remembered the godly old man's words, "Witness the first night."

I decided that I would let them all know that I was a Christian. I took out my large Bible, laid it open on my bed and got down on my knees. As soon as I closed my eyes to pray, a deathly hush descended on the billet. Singing, joking and playing stopped. I knew that all eyes were upon me. The silence was almost tangible. I felt awful. I wanted to open my eyes and look around me, but I was too embarrassed to do so. I kept my eyes closed and tried to pray. The only thing that kept me there was my determination. I was not really praying, but I wasn't going to give in and stop kneeling by my bedside. In any case, I did not really know what else to do.

My dilemma was soon solved for me. Someone threw a slipper. It hit me a glancing blow on the head and ricocheted off. The whole billet burst into laughter. The jokes and games resumed. My ordeal over I grinned and got into bed. I had shown them all that I was a Christian. From that night on, every morning and evening I knelt by my bedside to pray. The men in every billet I lived in during the next three years soon knew that I was a Christian, but it was all in my own strength.

I witnessed to my billet mates in other ways, too. I tried to interest them in the Christian message. On all-night guard duty, when two of us stood at the main gate sharing the same sentry box for hours on end and the other man had nowhere else to go, I tried to share my faith. I read my Bible every day. I prayed by my bedside for all to see. I tried to tell others of Christ. It was all to no avail. I was not able to lead one person to Christ. On the contrary, instead of attracting people to Christ I seemed to be turning them away.

This went on for about eighteen months. I had no real friends. I began to feel lonely, I played football for the camp team, captained the camp table tennis team and was the camp champion. Under normal circumstances this would have made a young man popular on a camp of three thousand men. In my case it did not. Sporting activities helped to alleviate my sense of loneliness but they did not cure it. I thought I was doing all the right things as a Christian, but my heart was growing colder and colder towards the Lord.

I enjoyed my work as an operations clerk in the control tower of a fighter command air force base. The long night duty could be boring, but in general I found the work interesting. We were even given the opportunity to fly in jet trainer aircraft from time to time. This enabled us to appreciate what it was like to receive messages from the control tower. I was very close to the town of Cambridge for most of my three years in the RAF. There were many interesting things to see and do there. The camp was only sixty miles from London, so I purchased a motorbike, taught myself how to ride it and made frequent weekend trips home.

During the football season I spent far less time in the control tower. Team members were relieved of duties to play in, and practice for, inter-camp matches. I also received time off for table tennis matches because the team represented the whole camp. When the squadron leader in charge of the control tower learned that I taught Sunday school in Deptford when I was home at weekends he was very impressed. He endeavoured to make sure that I got as many weekends off as possible to pursue this "highly commendable social activity which was a good example to other servicemen"! As far as it was possible to be happy doing national service I should have been content indeed, but all was not well with me.

After about eighteen months of trying hard to be a model Christian I began to slip back. I started to smoke again. I wanted to be 'one of the lads'. In my desire for company I started to attend the camp cinema. Being fighter command, there were no WAAF personnel on the camp. The camp cinema programmes seemed to reflect the absence of ladies! They were often far from wholesome. In the smoke-filled darkness, punctured by the occasional ribald remark and accompanying bursts of laughter; a small quiet voice within my heart would insistently whisper to me that I was a child of God, that I should not be there. Conviction grew stronger as the film progressed. I invariably left the cinema before the film was halfway through, sorry that I had gone in the first place.

I would return to the billet and read my Bible. Time after time I would come across words like the following:

*"Strengthened with might by his spirit in the inner man* (Eph. 3:16); *that Christ may dwell in your hearts by faith; that ye being rooted and grounded in love might be filled with all the fullness of God"* (Eph. 3:1719).

*"Now unto him that is able to do exceeding abundantly above all*

*that we ask or think, according to the power that worketh in us".* (Eph. 3:20).

*"Being filled with fruits of righteousness"* (Phil. 1:11).

The pages of the New Testament seemed to throb with joy, power, love and the thrill of being a Christian. It told of a quality of life that far exceeded my own Christian experience.

I was in a 'cleft stick'. I was enough of a Christian not to be able to enjoy a visit to the camp cinema, but I was a stranger to the kind of Christian life I read about in my New Testament. I felt I could not continue as I was. It had to be one or the other. Either I began to taste the Christian life I read about in my Bible or I give the whole thing up altogether, at least then I would be able to enjoy a smoke and sit all the way through a 'blue' film!

I began to seek God afresh. I knew the kind of Christian life I wanted. I did not want to drift away from my Lord. My prayer to the Lord at this time was, "Lord, if You will give me just a taste of the Christian life I read about in my New Testament, I will do anything and go anywhere for You."

I decided to spend as much time in prayer as possible. In the middle of the camp was a tiny, black, corrugated-iron church. It was rarely used, but often left open. I chose it as the place I would spend almost all my off duty hours seeking God. I set my heart on seeking till I found.

On the evening of the first day I made a list of all I had done that did not honour the Lord. I included my back-slidings, my pride and my self-effort. I wrote it all down, and confessed it all before the Lord in the quietness of the tiny church. I thought there might be some answer, some sign of approval, but there was none. I prayed on into the night. In the silent darkness my prayers seemed empty.

On the second day I again spent all my spare time in the church. By this time I was beseeching the Lord to show me what was wrong. I tried to trust Him, to receive from Him, but there seemed to be no answer.

On the third day I read passages from the New Testament and began to pray for the fullness of the Holy Spirit. By evening time I was reading specific passages of Scripture and seeking to exercise faith to receive. I read Luke 11:9-13, a passage which promises the Holy Spirit to all who ask for Him. I read such passages over and over again. In this way I tried to bolster my faith. Time after time I sought to come to a 'moment of faith' when I tried to receive. When I felt my faith was strong enough I would pray very deliberately, "Lord, I receive now!" but nothing happened.

I concluded my faith was not yet strong enough, so I read some more Scripture to make it stronger. I tried harder and harder to believe and receive, but all to no avail. Nothing happened. As soon as I stopped praying the silence remained unbroken. It seemed to mock me.

The darkness in the tiny church grew deeper and deeper as on and on I struggled, trying to become filled with the Holy Spirit. I began to despair. I had prayed so long. I had tried so hard. What more could I do?

While I knelt there, bewildered and disappointed, a verse of Scripture came into my mind. It was like a shaft of light, small at first but growing brighter. Within moments it illuminated my whole search. It gave me the answer to my bewilderment. Into my mind came the words of Jesus, *"What things soever ye desire, when ye pray, believe that ye receive them, and ye shall have them* (Mark 11:24)."

I rose from my knees, sure that my search had ended. It seemed so simple. I believed that I had received. In my heart was a quiet assurance that I was filled with the Holy Spirit. Nothing else had happened. The quietness of the tiny church remained unbroken. I walked through the darkness back to the billet. The billet was empty. The nine other airmen I shared it with were either still in town or on duty. I sat down in an armchair to read. I opened the book in my hands but never read a word. Quite suddenly my heart was filled with a deep sense of the presence of the Lord. My heart filled with a joy I could not contain. I leapt out of the chair and began to sing as I danced around the empty billet.

*"He lives! He lives! Christ Jesus lives today!*
*He walks with me, He talks with me along life's narrow way.*
*He lives! He lives! Salvation to impart! You ask me how I know He lives?*
*He lives within my heart"!*

I was filled with an assurance that Jesus Christ was alive, alive in me. It was as if a veil had been lifted from my mind, heart and spirit. I wept for joy. Jesus had manifested Himself to me and in me. I had tasted *'the joy unspeakable and full of glory'*.

I cannot recall whether I read my Bible and prayed the following morning. I suspect I did. What I do remember clearly was that I could not find my comb! This, to a young airman in the days in which we were known as the 'Brylcream boys', was a minor crisis. I did my best without a comb but went straight to the NAAFI shop to buy one before going on duty. When I opened the door of the shop I was met by the sound of loud music. The two girls from the local village who worked in the NAAFI shop had set up a record player on the counter and surrounded by the shelves of stationery, toilet articles and confectionery were jiving away to the sound of a 'rock and roll' band. As soon as I walked into the shop one of them stopped dancing and encouraged me to dance with her friend. They had been waiting for a man, any man! The ensuing conversation went something like this:

"Go on, dance!"

"Sorry, dear; but I don't dance."

"What's the matter with you then, got the hump or something?"

"No, no, not at all, I am very happy indeed. In actual fact I've never been so happy. My heart is full of joy!"

"What do you mean, full of joy?"

"I am really full of joy. It is difficult to explain but it certainly doesn't depend on whether I dance or not!"

"Can anyone have this joy?"

"Far as I know yes. Do you want to find real joy?"

"Yes, I do."

"All right, then, if you want to know how to have real joy, meet me at the little tin church in the middle of camp when I come off duty tonight"

"I'll be there."

That evening I went to the little church. She was waiting there. We went into the church together. I opened my Bible and explained the way of salvation to her. She listened intently. She said she understood. She knelt on the church floor and prayed, asking God to forgive her sin and make her a new person. She asked Christ into her heart and life.

I had been a Christian for three-and-a-half years. This was the first person I was enabled to lead to faith in Christ. It was not to be the last.

My experience the previous night had made a tremendous difference to me.

Shortly after this experience another Christian was posted, from another camp, into the billet. He, too, had recently sought for and received the fullness of the Holy Spirit. It was a great encouragement to me to have another Christian with whom to fellowship and share. We commenced a Bible study in the little tin church under the auspices of the Soldiers' and Airmen's Scripture Readers Association. In this way we sought to witness to our colleagues on the camp. My new found friend also became my first prayer partner. He and his wife have prayed for our ministry from the very first day I started training for the mission field.

Though I felt that life was unfair to me when I discovered I was among the very last group of young men called up for national service, I can now look back with much thankfulness and rejoicing. My extremity had become His opportunity. I was about to discover what the Lord's plan for me was. Even the coming of a fellow-Christian into the billet was all part of that plan.

Chapter Three

# THE PLAN UNFOLDS

A few weeks before I knelt on the kitchen floor in my friend's home the mission hall appointed its first fulltime pastor. Until then the leadership and ministry had been directed by a dedicated band of men and women who gave most of their free time to evangelism in Deptford. Most of them lived in the suburbs of southeast London or in the county of Kent.

George and Anna Roberts were from Northern Ireland. They came to London to attend a missionary candidates' course. They hoped to serve with the Christian Literature Crusade in South America, but were turned down on medical grounds. Instead of going to South America they came to Deptford, southeast London. They brought their missionary vision and burden with them. They prayed fervently for us young people. Though we were Christians many of us knew very little about victorious Christian living. George and Anna recognised this immediately. They loved us and wept over us because they desired God's best for us. The mission hall had many dedicated leaders who also loved us and gave of their time unstintingly, but because they were not on the spot they were not always accessible.

George and Anna Roberts lived in a tiny flat above the mission hall. They were always available, and they won our hearts in very practical ways. George was not the most gifted of footballers! However, he would always turn out for us if we were a man short, even if it meant leaving his sermon preparation. If we needed help or advice of any kind we knew he was always there. If we dropped in at meal times Anna always laid another place. If we visited late at night there was always hot tea and buttered toast. Even when they had three young children of their own we were always made welcome. When the Lord met with me in the Royal Air Force I did not need to tell George and Anna. They recognised the change immediately.

Above all, George and Anna trained us young people for Christian service. It was in their little flat that we learned what it was to pray through the night. I cannot recall any of George's sermons on prayer, but I can remember him praying as he poured out his heart for us and the other young people under his pastoral care. He was also humble enough to ask us to pray for him and his wife. They did not find life in Deptford easy. It was so different to Northern Ireland. We prayed for them as they prayed for us.

George Roberts also taught us evangelism. Under his leadership we were encouraged to take the message of Christ into the streets. On Saturday mornings we sold the *Challenge* newspaper and the Christian magazine for West Indians, *Caribbean Challenge,* in the local market place. We had to shout to compete with the quick-witted and silver-tongued stall holders who tried to talk the crowds into buying anything from 'Parisian perfumes' to alarm clocks and china ornaments. It was not easy to stand and shout amidst the crowds who thronged the secondhand clothing stalls and barrows piled high with all manner of interesting junk The hardest part was being seen by family members and former friends. For the most part we did not sell many newspapers and magazines. It would have been easy to give up, but George and Anna Roberts had the gift of encouragement, and so we continued.

On Saturday nights we often went into the pubs in the High Street to distribute tracts and sell Christian booklets. We had to compete with the boisterous singing, the talkative drunks and the occasional belligerent who greeted us with, "Clear off! I don't want religion pushed down me froat while I'm 'aving me beer!" (which was quite reasonable seeing we had invaded his territory!). As we moved from table to table with booklets and tracts I sometimes met old friends with whom I had played football in the past. Invariably they would greet me warmly, and offer to 'buy me a pint'. Most publicans were quite willing to allow us into their pubs for short periods. Most of the customers gladly received something to read, but I always went in fear and trembling. There were very real dangers around the pubs in Deptford High Street late on Saturday nights. All the same, we went. After we had visited our last pub our next stop would be the fish and chip shop. We would each buy a bag of chips wrapped in newspaper to keep the chips warm. We soaked them with liberal sprinklings of malt vinegar plus lots of salt. Chips in hand we made our way back to the mission hall, glad that our pub visitation was over, but happy that we had told others of Christ. Such fellowship has a flavour all its own!

George Roberts also taught us how to preach, both inside and outside the mission hall. His methods were unorthodox but effective. At the Young People's Fellowship on Saturday nights he would place an open-air preaching stand at the front of the hall. He then called upon young people, without any warning, to come to the front, step up onto the preaching stand and talk without stopping on any subject they liked for two minutes. At other times he would pick a subject for us. It could be anything from London Transport to doughnuts! We then progressed to giving short, five-minute testimonies in front of the other young people, while they were encouraged to heckle and play the role of drunks by throwing pennies and other objects in the direction of the speaker. Thus trained, we often preached and testified in the open air before bus queues, cinema queues and all kinds of drunks and rowdies.

His method of training us to preach inside the mission hall was a little more sophisticated but none the less unorthodox. He would choose any of us he thought were likely preachers and inform us that we were to preach to the Young People's Fellowship on a certain date. The first time he told me to preach he simply said, "Pat, I would like you to preach to the YPF in six weeks' time. Preach for twenty minutes on Mary and Martha (Luke 10:38-42). Here is something to help you. Come to me for any further help at any time."

It was not so much a request, but on the other hand it was not a command. One got the impression that an honour was being bestowed rather than a task given. The thought of refusing never entered my head. If George Roberts thought I could do it then I would try.

He slipped into my hand a single sheet of paper which was headed Landsdowne Bible Study Notes. On it was the outline of a sermon on Mary and Martha. With this as my basis I began to prepare. I read the passage many times, referred to some books from George Robert's bookshelves and prepared a twenty-minute sermon. I was ready with weeks to spare. I set about memorising my sermon word for word. I made sure it took exactly twenty minutes. I knew that at the Young People's Fellowship all present would be asked to evaluate the sermon. I wanted to keep such evaluation to the minimum.

By the time the Saturday to preach arrived I had memorised my sermon word perfect. We had a football match on Blackheath that Saturday afternoon. As we walked up the hill to the heath I asked one of my friends to listen to, and time, my sermon. I recited it to him. It took exactly twenty minutes! That evening I preached for the first time. At the conclusion the first question was, "Why did you only preach for twelve minutes?" I was so nervous I had recited my sermon at almost twice the intended speed!

We made many mistakes but George and Anna were patient with us. I looked forward to my weekends in Deptford while I saw out the last eighteen months of my three years in the Royal Air Force.

George Robert's method of training bore fruit. By the time I got to Missionary Training College I had already seen people come to Christ through preaching, as well as through personal witnessing. I had even seen my mother weeping in the congregation as I preached the gospel at the mission hall. One of my sisters became a Sunday School teacher. She even studied sign language in order to teach the deaf.

It was George and Anna Roberts who first sowed the seeds of missionary vision in my heart.

I never forgot the prayer I prayed when I decided to seek the Lord's blessing on my life, "Lord, if You will give me just a taste of New Testament Christianity I will go anywhere and do anything for You" I began to pray earnestly about my future. My job at Crosse & Blackwell was being kept for me. I naturally assumed I would return to it once I was finished in the Royal Air Force. I had, in fact, devised a plan for my future. First I would study for more O levels and A levels. I would then take the accountancy exams. I would earn a good salary, move out of Deptford, buy a little house in the suburbs, marry a Christian girl and then commute to the mission hall to teach and serve.

I had never prayed much about this. I assumed it would all be good and pleasing to the Lord. It was a pattern many had followed. There was little wrong with my plan. In fact, there was only one thing wrong with it; it was *my* plan for my life. Now I began to see things differently. I began to ask the lord what I should do with my life. I was truly willing to do anything.

I read avidly the lives of famous Christians. The stories of men like David Brainerd, Robert Murray McCheyne, Johnathan Edwards, Andrew Bonar, Hudson Taylor and C.T. Studd became my meat and drink. I could not imagine how I could have possibly preferred the camp cinema to those wonderful books. In my spare time I sat and read for hour after hour, thrilled at the lives of men who had truly brought honour to the name of Christ.

In my zeal I even began to copy some of the things they had done. I decided to fast every Tuesday, because I read in one of the biographies that fasting was a secret of spiritual power. All went well for the first few weeks. I hurried to the mess hall after evening duty and tucked into a hearty meal, my only one of the day. After the first month I bought one bar of chocolate in the morning so that I could eat it at the stroke of four (the time I had set myself to fast to). It wasn't long before I found myself counting the seconds on the clock. I popped the first square of chocolate into my mouth as soon as the clock struck four!

I stopped feeling very spiritual after that. I wondered if John Wesley ever had such troubles! I was learning that the Lord had not called me to copy others.

During this time I was waiting for God to speak to me about my future. Four months after the Lord met with me in the little tin church on the camp, I read a small paperback book entitled *Mission Fields Today*. It was published by the InterVarsity Press. It was simply a collection of surveys describing the spiritual needs of the countries of the world. Page after page told of country after country with so few Christians and little, if any, witness to Christ. It was not an emotional account. On the contrary it was more a collection of bare facts and statistics, but by the time I finished that book I knew I would not return to my job at Crosse & Blackwell. I knew I was called to be a missionary. The thought thrilled me. I no longer dreamed of my little house in the suburbs. Through reading that book I exchanged an earthly dream for a heavenly vision. I was to be a missionary.

I spoke to George Roberts. I told him that I thought I was called to the mission field. We prayed together. He assured me that God would confirm this call through His Word. The following morning I read from the J.B.Phillips' translation of the New Testament. These were the words given to me:

*"God has done His part see that you do yours ... Set your minds then on endorsing, by your conduct, the fact that God has called and chosen you".*

Though slightly out of context, these words were a confirmation of God's call to me.

The following morning I went to the only place I had ever met a missionary, the Christian Literature Crusade bookshop in Ludgate Hill. Books had played a crucial part in my Christian life. This, combined with what I had heard through George Roberts, led me to ask at the CLC shop how I could become a missionary with the Christian Literature Crusade. I was promptly told that I should apply for missionary training at the Worldwide Evangelization Crusade missionary training college in Glasgow.

I applied to the college and was informed that I could start the two-year course in January the following year. So it was that two weeks after being de-mobbed from the RAF, I arrived on the doorstep of the WEC missionary training college. I was dressed in my only suit. I carried a battered suitcase which held all I possessed. In my pocket were just a few pounds of de-mob money from the RAF.

My father had declared me a fool for not going back to my old job at Crosse & Blackwell but my mother, being more aware of the great change which had taken place in my life, said, "If that's what you want, son, you go ahead. You do what will make you happiest"

I had embarked upon what I later learned was known as 'a life of faith'. I had to trust the Lord to supply all I needed for fees and living expenses. I did not have a government grant. In actual fact, it never even occurred to me to apply for one. The only regular means of support I had was a monthly gift from the friend I made in the RAF and the occasional gift from the mission hall in Deptford. But none of this gave me any cause for concern. The thrill of training to be a missionary filled both my heart and mind. There was no room to doubt that He would provide all I needed. He never failed to do so.

The missionary training college consisted of two large four-storey houses on the corner of a quiet street in west Glasgow. All the surrounding houses were large. There were plenty of trees and shrubbery in all the front gardens. Over the gateway that stood before the short pathway which led to the steps leading up to the front door; in wrought iron letters were the reassuring words, 'Have Faith in God'. I climbed the steps to the front door. I was filled with excitement. I knew I was doing something which God had clearly led me to do. I rang the doorbell and waited.

The door was opened by a scholarly-looking gentleman. He wore spectacles which seemed to be perched on the tip of his nose. He was a little 'thin on top'. He greeted me with the words, "You must be Patrick. We are expecting you". He knew my name. I was impressed and felt pleasantly at ease. I was to learn later that I had been welcomed by the principal.

Coming straight from billet life in the RAF, life at the missionary training college was like stepping into a different world. The house was very different to the only other really large house I had ever entered, the reception centre in Chelsea. Here there was no gloom. Although it was the largest house I had ever been in, it was not a sense of space that impressed me but rather a sense of peace and warmth. There were about fifty students at the college: thirty young ladies and twenty young men. They were from all walks of life: teachers, mechanics, farmers, doctors, nurses and clerks. There was even a policeman, a chef, and a theologian from Germany.

A good night's sleep in a downstairs room shared with four others was followed by breakfast in a dining room shared by both staff and students. Then came my first academic task, an IQ test. I did my best and was told afterwards that I had scored well. Because of this a high standard of work would be expected of me! Each student's work was assessed according to his or her IQ. I wished I had not been so lucky with my answers.

My first prayer letter to my friends back in Deptford reflected my impressions of the missionary training college after I had been there for a few weeks.

January 1962

*"I do thank you for your prayers. It is a real joy to be here. There is so much to praise the Lord for. The study of God's Word is a real joy, and we have so much time for study. The fellowship is just grand. One sings while peeling potatoes, cleaning windows and travelling on the tube train around Glasgow! We have grand times at the open-air meetings each Sunday afternoon in a large Glasgow marketplace".*

Life at the training college was filled with variety. Study included theology, motor mechanics, Bible doctrines, English grammar, Greek, music, and homiletics. Practical tasks included painting and decorating, 'spud bashing', cooking, washing up and carpentry. We did our own laundry in teams. We played volleyball and football for exercise and relaxation. The day began at 6.30am and ended at 9.00pm. Evangelism was practised rather than taught and was conducted in an atmosphere of prayer and faith. Extracts from my early prayer letters reveal this clearly.

February 1962

*We are praising the Lord, for He is at work through the fellowship. People are finding the Saviour through the door-to-door visitation, during weekend meetings in churches, and through the open-air witness. So far this term over 40 have been saved and others contacted through these ministries.*

April 1962
*The term got off to a good start. At the first open-air meeting in the
market place an old man of seventy-seven asked Jesus into his heart,
three of us having the privilege of praying with him in the street.
Praise the Lord with us!*

June 1962
*Last weekend we had quite an Acts of the Apostles' open-air meeting.
A good crowd listened to the testimonies, music and message. At the
end many came forward in recognition of their need to know the way
of salvation. They took tracts and booklets to read in the quietness of
their own homes. Afterwards many were contacted personally.
We had opposition from an atheist who started preaching against us.
The crowd grew as the college students were giving out portions of
the Word of God, whilst another, an ex-marine engineer from
Hartlepool, continued with his testimony The atheist tried hard to
convince the crowd that the testimony was a figment of the student's
imagination, but he only succeeded in drawing more people to come
and listen. As a result of his opposition many more came to receive
Scripture portions.*

November 1962
*We rejoice here at the college for souls saved. Each week people are
being saved in ones and twos through the open-air ministry, visitation
and church meetings. So far this term ten have found the Saviour.*

My most exciting experience in evangelism whilst at college came in
my second year as a student. Divided into groups of five or six, we
were formed into evangelistic teams which were sent to churches all
over Scotland. Each team was based at a church for three weeks. It
was my privilege to lead a team based at a Baptist church in the town
of Wishaw near Motherwell. We were certainly a mixed bunch. Davey
had been a marine engineer, Derek had been a shipyard electrician.
Both were training to become missionaries to Thailand. Sven-Arne
was from Sweden and heading for Chile. Our fifth member was Jack,
an ex-policeman from Liverpool. We were particularly pleased that
Jack was in our team because he was the best barber in the college

and money was scarce!

The college gave each team twenty pounds which we were expected to pay back upon our return. We slept on camp beds in the church hall, and were fed sumptously by the ladies of the church who worked to a rota and tried to outdo each other in terms of taste and volume! I had never eaten so well in my life!

Mornings were spent in prayer and Bible study, while afternoons were spent doing door-to-door visitation, open-air meetings in the High Street, and personal evangelism. In the evenings we conducted evangelistic meetings in the church hall. We named these meetings, "The Late Night Special". They began at around 9.30pm and were designed to attract young people from off the streets and from the pubs.

We had a great time in Wishaw. The church welcomed and encouraged us. We in turn gave ourselves wholeheartedly to the task. Each night the church hall was filled with young people. As the days progressed more and more young people came to the late night meeting. Unknown to us, a strong criminal element also began to attend. Deacons' coats hanging in the church hall entrance were slashed with razor blades. Some young men came full of drink. Cigarette ends began to litter the church hall. Some deacons, sensing danger and worried about the safety of the ladies of the church, moved that the meetings be discontinued. Others declared that these young people might never enter the church again and concluded that we should grasp this opportunity to reach them whatever the cost. The latter prevailed and the meetings continued.

We ourselves were from the factory, the shipyards, the council estates and the street corners. Davey had been a 'teddy-boy' and a street fighter himself. We knew the language of these young people, we knew how they thought. Our backgrounds were similar.

We were getting through to these young people but, unbeknown to us, we were also hurting the unity of one of the more vicious gangs in Wishaw. Consequently, the leaders of this gang decided to attend the Late Night Special with the intention of attacking the team and putting a stop to the meetings.

The seats at the Late Night Special were arranged in a large semicircle.

Whoever was speaking or testifying did not use a lectern or a table but simply roamed around inside the semicircle speaking in a natural way to the audience.

The rest of the team sat behind the speaker facing the audience. Our would be attackers occupied the very front row ready to pretend to answer the appeal. Their leader planned to come forward first. This would be the signal for them all to attack. Some carried knives which they planned to use.

Davey, the ex-marine engineer, gave a powerful testimony of how Jesus Christ had changed his life. This was followed by a simple gospel message which applied the good news of Christ and his love for us. An appeal was made. Immediately the gang leader came forward only to fall on his knees and begin to confess his sins. His mates thought he was joking and waited for the signal to attack. It never came.

Slowly it dawned upon them that their leader was not larking about. He was at the front weeping!

What a time we had, as one young man after another came forward and asked for counselling. Many wept their way to the cross and gave their hearts to Christ. It was only afterwards that we heard of the danger we had been in.

In all, twenty-four young people and adults came to Christ. One of the older young men sold his shotgun in order to go on holiday with the church young people. Another young man, with a reputation of violence all over the town, was so changed that he became a target for retaliation from the many enemies he had made over the years. Yet another is now a minister of the gospel himself. It was wonderful for us young men training for the mission field to see the power of the Holy Spirit in evangelism during these three weeks. It was missionary training of the highest order. We returned to the college rejoicing.

One other aspect of training we practised rather than studied was the ministry of prayer. We spent many hours praying for missionaries overseas. The college was a centre of up-to-date information from all over the world. Former students were serving as missionaries on all five continents. Letters from them contained news of the great challenges and dangers of missionary service. At times we were called from our studies to pray for missionaries in danger, or those facing sudden crises. This was all part of our training. We were being taught to count the cost of long-term missionary service.

One of my early prayer letters from college describes the effect the news of missionaries in danger had upon me.

May 1962

*'I have decided to follow Jesus... No turning back, no turning back'*
*I sang these words yesterday at a children's meeting. As I sang I began to wonder where I might be called to follow. It is a sobering thought considering that even just this week we had news of a missionary shot in Thailand. There is so much unrest in the world today, especially in parts of the world where missionaries serve. I do not know yet where the Lord would have me go for Him but praise His Name, I believe I am willing to go anywhere. I fully realise that these may appear presumptuous words, but I know He is able not only to lead me and guide me, but also to keep and sustain me if I but trust Him completely.*
*Another chorus often sung is, 'My Lord knows the way through the wilderness, all I have to do is to follow' That is all, 'follow'. It seems so simple, yet I am sure I do not realise what following Jesus really means. More and more it is being impressed upon me that I must go the way of the cross. This means giving all we have, our plans, possessions even perhaps our lives as we submit to His will. That's all, just follow! Please pray that I might have the grace and strength to do just that and, of course, pray it for yourself too!*

Not long after writing this a young Worldwide Evangelization Crusade missionary family in Vietnam had their house blown up by a terrorist bomb. The bomb was planted under the house while the parents and their two little daughters slept inside. Both parents were injured and had to be flown back to Scotland immediately. The two little girls were miraculously unharmed. When we sang 'No turning back' at the missionary training college we had to really mean it.

The staff at the college taught us to pray by praying with us.

Intercession for missionaries overseas, and for our own evangelism in the Glasgow docks, on the streets and in the churches, supplication for the daily needs of the college, praise and thanksgiving for answered prayer was all undertaken by staff and students praying together. The missionary training college was indeed a school of prayer.

In addition to praying for missionaries and our own evangelism, the leader of the Worldwide Evangelization Crusade work in Scotland and the founder of the college, Mr Rowbotham, urged us to join him in praying for the provision of a conference centre for WEC in Scotland. He testified that he believed WEC Britain needed its own conference centre where the missionary challenge could be presented in a variety of different ways. We all knew there was no money to buy such a place, but such niceties were of no concern to Mr Rowbotham. As far as he was concerned the conference centre was already ours. We just could not see it yet!

Urged on by the faith of Mr Rowbotham and his wife, we, too, prayed for the fulfillment of this vision. I was absolutely amazed when one morning he told us we need pray no more for the conference centre. He had found the place. A beautiful conference centre standing in its own grounds on the banks of the Firth of Clyde. He then proceeded to tell us students that our prayers had been answered. The owners had given it to him for nothing! The place was just an hour's drive from the college. I had never known such things were possible, but it was all true. A church in southeast London had been given the place, but it was too far for them to use regularly. They heard of Mr Rowbotham's vision, and it was his for nothing!

Shortly afterwards we students were transported in teams to the new conference centre, Kilcreggan House, armed with hammers, saws, screwdrivers and paint brushes. It was our task to extend and improve the conference centre given in answer to 'our' prayers.

Never had I heard anyone pray like Mr Rowbotham. He was like a child before God. He simply told the Lord he needed timber, paint, nails, and a host of different materials. He named them one by one, respectfully reminding the Lord that it was His work. He then gave thanks for the materials and acted as if he already had them! I was amazed, but before long I would be among the students taken out to

Kilcreggan House to bang in the nails and saw the timber he had prayed for.

While at the training college I also spent my summer holidays at the conference centre. Week after week the conference centre was filled with visitors from all over the British Isles. They came to hear Bible ministry from gifted speakers and missionaries from all over the world, while they enjoyed a good holiday in Scotland. We students served by doing many of the practical tasks necessary at such a place. We were also given regular opportunities to testify and share in the meetings. As a result of this, many people committed themselves to pray for us.

The very atmosphere of the training college and the conference centre seemed to me to be permeated with faith and prayer. As far as I was concerned, I felt I was being given the best possible training for the mission field I could find anywhere.

When my two years were over I applied to stay for another year but to no avail. In December of 1963, my last month at the college, I wrote to those who were praying for me,

Dear Friends,

*This will be my last letter from the missionary training college. It is difficult to assess what God has done for me during these two years but I have this testimony He has never failed you or me. I say 'you or me' because it is my conviction that any testimony I may have really belongs as much to those of you who pray for me, as to myself. But ultimately our testimony is only ours because of the faithfulness of God. Join me in praise to Him. There are two principles that have been thoroughly impressed upon me in the last two years. The first concerns the will of God, the second the Word of God.*

*1. I knew that my salvation was the will of God. I have learned that the will of God is my salvation. This is proved every time anyone steps outside the will of God for their lives. I do not mean that a disobedient Christian is no longer saved, but I have learned that there is no present enjoyment of salvation's blessings outside the revealed will of God for my life. Therefore the secret of blessing is obedience to God's revealed will for my life.*

*2. The Word of God. I have discovered that to receive the Word of God into my mind makes me think. To receive the Word of God into my heart or emotions makes me rejoice or cry. However, to receive the Word of God into my spirit makes me think and act, and that not without emotion.*

*I have discovered that the Word of God rightly received becomes a driving force and a guiding principle, rather than a text book to be studied in order to learn about the state of the lost or the truth of the trinity.*

*It is no help to the lost simply that I know they are lost.*

*I can receive the Word of God intellectually and know about the lost. I can receive the Word of God emotionally and cry about the lost. However, it is not until one receives the truth spiritually that one, not only knows and cries, but also goes. (Either in prayer or presence we must go to the lost.)*

*If only I could fully learn these two lessons I would gladly spend another two years here in college, but now I must put into practice what I have learned.*

By the time I left the college I knew where I should serve as a missionary. I was called to Japan. There was nothing spectacular or dramatic about this call. After I had been at the college for one year I realised that if I knew which country I was heading for I would be able to prepare myself in a more specific manner. I made it a habit to regularly and frequently pray concerning the country in which I would serve as a missionary. At the college there were missionary speakers from all over the world, but I never heard anyone speak about Japan. It was somewhat of a surprise to me that as I prayed one day the land of Japan came into my mind. I simply told the Lord that if He wanted me to go there, then I would go.

From that time on, every time I prayed about the future the land of Japan came into my mind. This went on for some months, so I decided to tell another of the students that I thought perhaps the Lord was calling me to Japan. As soon as I did this I experienced a deep peace in my heart. I became increasingly sure that I was called to Japan.

*Patrick at the age of 25, after leaving the Missionary Training College.*

As I continued to pray and express my willingness before the lord, the conviction that this was indeed the pathway I should tread grew stronger still. Eventually, at one of the monthly missionary conferences at the college, I testified publicly that I had become increasingly confident that God was calling me to Japan. Upon doing this the sense of peace and conviction that this was God's will for me became complete. From that time forward I never doubted my call to Japan. I saw many other prayers answered at college. All my needs were supplied. I was enabled to pay the last few pounds of my fees just a few days before I left.

There was one prayer which, thankfully, remained unanswered! It was a prayer that I began to pray towards the beginning of my second year at the college. The college, though a place of joy and faith, was also a place of strict discipline. No more was this evident than in the rules which governed the relationship between male and female students. Personal communication between male and female students could only take place at the meal table where a staff member was always present. Even the lecture hall-cum-study was divided by a wooden partition which was only partly removed for lectures to the whole student body. Volleyball was never played in mixed groups. Male students were not even allowed to watch female students play. Meeting outside the college was also strictly forbidden.

These rules were all part of our training for life in other cultures where we would need to be far more circumspect and adaptable in our personal relationships. Some students felt the rules were too restrictive, others said they thought them old-fashioned, while to others they presented a challenge! A few 'smitten' students invented ingenious ways of circumventing the rules. At times, upon opening an obscure theological tome in the library, a little note of affection would fall out. Such notes were normally at the end of the book. They were often quite meaningless to any but the person they were intended for.

The rules suited me just fine. I was very determined not to let anything distract me from my training and preparation. The knowledge that the Lord was calling me to Japan made me even more determined not to countenance anything that would keep me from concentrating on the task at hand.

Imagine my concern then, when I began to find it difficult to concentrate, especially during prayer times. Thoughts about one of the young lady students began to enter my mind unannounced! She had entered the college towards the end of my first year. Whenever I got alone to pray or think my mind turned to her! I tried to discipline myself more strongly. I prayed fervently against every thought of her. I was convinced that any distraction at such a stage in my training could only be wrong and not of God. At times I thought I had succeeded. I avoided her studiously being careful never to sit at the same table and not to be in sight of her when we all met as a student body for prayer or lectures. However, no matter how hard I tried to drive her out of my mind, I was unsuccessful.

This struggle went on for months until one day as I prayed, the hitherto unthought-of-possibility that perhaps the Lord was trying to tell me something dawned upon me!

As soon as I was finished at the college I wrote her a letter telling her how I felt. Being a very perceptive young lady she had known for months! My very disciplined approach of studiously ignoring her had been a confirmation to her that my feelings towards her reciprocated hers toward me. Four years later Sarah and I were married in a little Japanese church in the suburbs of Tokyo. I have been grateful ever since that the Lord did not answer my prayers for the ability to cast every thought of her from my mind!

Chapter Four
# ON THE WAY

---

I left the training college towards the end of December 1963. I went home to Deptford to spend Christmas there. By 1 January I had moved to the London headquarters of the Christian Literature Crusade, a missionary society with literature work all over the world. There I began a period of fifteen months' further preparation, training to be a literature missionary These were very busy months. We studied literature evangelism, bookshop management, warehousing and distribution. I learned to drive, how to pack books, and how to introduce Christian literature to others in a variety of interesting ways. I enjoyed the work immensely, especially when appointed to work in the bookshop at Ludgate Hill to gain experience. It was a place I had come to love and appreciate as a young Christian.

At the shop the day began with prayer and tidying up. Prayer always included intercession for customers who did not know Christ as Saviour. There were many opportunities to speak to such customers concerning their need of Christ. Some put their faith in Him right there in the shop.

It was during this time of preparation that I set foot inside a university for the first time. The missionary society needed to know whether I was likely to be able to tackle the difficult Japanese language with any possibility of success. I was sent to the School of Oriental and African Studies at London University to sit a language aptitude test. I did not look forward to it.

The day to go to the university arrived. As I approached the imposing Senate House building I felt ill at ease. Inside the School of Oriental and African Studies I felt like an impostor. Students hurried here and there carrying armfuls of books and papers. Lecturers walked by in their gowns. I felt very much out of place. I did not have a clue what to expect. I was quite overwhelmed by the occasion. The uniformed commissionaire directed me to the office of a professor of Japanese. I was told to go in, sit down and wait.

The office was lined with books in Japanese. Their spines and covers displayed a confusing array of Chinese characters. A heavy sense of learning  pervaded the room. I felt intensely inferior. I had failed O level French at school. The professor knew that my four O level passes contained no languages at all. He also knew that I had never sat an A level examination. I had no idea at all what a language aptitude test consisted of. I waited nervously for the professor to come. When he entered the room I stood hesitatingly to my feet. I did not know what else to do.

The professor was a kind man. He spoke gently to me. He did his best to put me at ease. My nervousness must have been painfully obvious. The test began. The professor proceeded to string together a series of unintelligible sounds at what seemed to me an alarming speed. He then asked me to repeat them after him. I felt ridiculous as I spluttered out what I thought I had heard. He then made some more noises. Again I tried to repeat them. This went on for about ten minutes. He was probably speaking Japanese, of which I did not know one word. The professor did not seem very impressed with my efforts.

Next I was handed a sheet of paper. On it were written some sentences in what I can only presume was Japanese written in the English alphabet. There were gaps in the sentences here and there. The professor called my attention to the gaps. He then instructed me to fill them in with I what I thought were appropriate words by comparing one sentence with the others. I soon wished I was back spluttering unintelligible sounds again! The exercise did not make sense to me at all. I made a few guesses. I hoped they were inspired but feared they were not.

I came away despondent and discouraged. The assessment sent to the mission leaders was not good. It declared that I would find Japanese language study very difficult. It concluded that I might not really get the language at all.

Upon hearing the result of the assessment test I assured the mission leadership that God had called me to Japan. I promised them I would work hard at the language. I was told I could go forward to Japan providing I first attended a six-week course of basic linguistics organised by the Wycliffe Bible Translators. I attended the course at an ex-RAF camp in southeast England. There were over 100 missionary candidates from various missionary societies on the course. I did my best and studied hard but my marks were not impressive. However by the end of the course I at least knew what the professor at London University was getting at!

I was not aware of it at the time but the six weeks' basic linguistics course changed my whole outlook towards language study. Above all, I was no longer afraid of the Japanese language.

One other major event took place before I sailed to Japan. Sarah and I became engaged. Sarah had finished her two years at the missionary training college and had moved down to the London HQ of the Christian Literature Crusade to continue her preparation for missionary service in Japan. I was to leave for Japan first and Sarah was to follow one year later. Getting engaged before I left seemed to us to be a good idea.

However, getting engaged was one thing, buying a ring was another! God had proved His faithfulness to me while at the training college. I had been enabled to pay all my fees without a grant. Life at the Christian Literature Crusade was on the same 'faith' basis. We trusted God for our living expenses and contributed to a common pool. No one received any allowance from the mission. I had never lacked financially, but on the other hand I had not been able to save.

I decided to spend every penny I possessed on a ring for Sarah. This was not a difficult decision to make because I only had eleven pounds! With this in hand I went to a jewellers in Deptford High Street. I asked to see some engagement rings. The jeweller immediately produced a number of trays of diamond rings.

They all looked very beautiful. They were all very expensive, far beyond the eleven pounds I had in my pocket. In response to my lack of enthusiasm the jeweller respectfully asked how much I was prepared to pay for an engagement ring. Upon hearing my reply, "Eleven pounds," he put all the trays he had intended to show me back into their respective places and then produced what must have been the cheapest diamond ring in the shop. The diamond was so small you could hardly see it. It cost just eleven pounds. I bought and took it home for everyone to see.

Mother exclaimed, "It's lovely! Very nice!" (Mother would have said the same had it cost one pound or ten thousand pounds.)

My brothers crowded round to look at it "The ring's all right but when are you going back for the diamond? We can't see it anywhere!" they proclaimed with grins all over their faces.

Father declared that he could just catch a glimpse of the diamond if the light shone on it from the right direction. He then asked how much it cost. Upon hearing it cost eleven pounds he said, "Must be a U.G.B. diamond at that price!"

*Farewell at Warterloo Station 1965*

"What's a U.G.B. diamond, dad?" everyone inquired, only to be told with a chuckle that U.G.B. were the initials for United Glass Bottles! All had a good laugh at my expense but Sarah accepted the ring and has been happy with it ever since.

The fellowship at the Shaftesbury Society mission hall in Deptford was very generous to me. With gifts from them and other friends my passage to Japan was paid. The date was set for me to leave Britain on board a P & O passenger liner from Southampton to Yokohama. It was both a daunting and yet exciting prospect. I had never left the British Isles before. The longest journey I had ever made on a passenger boat was the ferry trip over to the Isle of Wight for the Boy's Brigade camps. Now I was about to go to the other side of the world.

I spent my last few days in Britain with my family in Deptford. I packed my trunk and said goodbye to my friends. On the 12th March 1965 I started my journey. My brothers and sisters went off to school or work as usual, each with a cheery "Goodbye, Pat. Look after yourself over there."

Father's farewell words were "Goodbye, son. I don't think I will ever see you again". (Father died six months later while waiting at Charing Cross Station for his train home from work).

Only mother accompanied me to Waterloo Station. There, friends from the mission hall and the Christian Literature Crusade mission HQ had gathered to give me a send off. While we waited for the train to Southampton to leave we prayed and sang hymns on the platform. Commuters did not quite know what to make of us, neither did the railway staff.

Tears from mother, a hug from Sarah, handshakes and words of encouragement from my friends and I was on my way. The train pulled out slowly from the station. I was now on my own, on my way to Japan. I had become a missionary.

The huge white and gold P & O liner berthed at Southampton was indeed an imposing sight. I had never seen such a huge ship at close quarters before, let alone board one. The dockside was a hive of activity as passengers boarded, luggage was loaded and fond farewells made on the quayside.

Once on board I was met by a steward and shown to my cabin. I was interested to know what kind of person I was sharing the cabin with. My cabin-mate turned out to be a missionary, an Irishman from the Brethren Assemblies in Belfast. His name was Willie and he was heading for Korea. He, too, was a 'first-timer'. We discovered, too, that we had been allotted seats at the same dining table.

Once the voyage began each passenger was shown to his or her table in the huge dining room. We were told that we would be at the same table for the whole journey The steward encouraged us to introduce ourselves to our fellow passengers and get to know one another.

Introductions began. I listened carefully and tried to remember the names of the other seven passengers at the table. There was a teacher on her way to Hong Kong, a nurse heading for Singapore and a French lady travelling to Japan to join her husband. Each passenger gave name and occupation. When it came to my cabin-mate's turn he gave his name and then to my surprise announced himself as an ambassador! Everyone seemed most impressed. He continued, "I am an ambassador from Ireland on my way to Korea".

One or two of the passengers looked a little perplexed, obviously wondering what such a fellow was doing in the economy class dining room. He then concluded, "I am an ambassador for the Lord Jesus Christ!"

I was very impressed with his enthusiasm, but doubted his wisdom. Our table-mates did not know where to look. One could almost hear them thinking, "We've got a right one here!"

Finally it was my turn to introduce myself. When I simply said that I, too, was a missionary my introduction somehow fell flat. I did not sense that our table-mates were too enthusiastic at the prospect of having to eat at a table three times a day with two missionaries present all the time. However, they were stuck with us for five weeks.

Willie and I soon discovered that there were over twenty missionaries on the liner. Some of them had already planned Bible studies and fellowship meetings for the evenings.

It was exciting for me to discover on the boat that the Lord's family is a large and interesting family! While the majority of the passengers wined and dined and danced each night after the evening meal, about twenty of us began to meet for praise and Bible study. Very soon Christian members of the crew joined us and our numbers began to swell. At times there were as many as forty enjoying the singing and the fellowship. I enjoyed these times very much, especially as I had not expected there to be anything like this on the ship. My cabinmate and I became good friends, and together we made many more friends at the evening meetings. When the fellowship times were over we enjoyed the coolness of the open deck where we could stroll and play deck games, or just relax in the deck chairs and talk while we listened to the strains of the orchestra as they played for those dancing in the ballroom. The journey of a lifetime had begun.

Soon after we left Southampton we met a violent storm in the Bay of Biscay. The huge liner heaved to and fro. It was difficult to keep one's feet on the deck. We were warned not to go on to the outer decks while the storm persisted. Most passengers would not have attempted it anyway. They were horizontal, on their beds in their cabins. I did not realise this until I went to the dining room for the evening meal. In the huge dining room, where normally hundreds sat waiting to be served, there were less than a dozen scattered here and there. It was an impressive sight to see all the waiters in their allotted places as if the dining room was full of hungry people! Willie and I were the only ones at our table. We tucked in as usual, but we paid for it later! We soon joined the horizontal passengers!

Once we entered the Mediterranean Sea the more pleasant part of the journey began. The sun shone. In every direction the calm sea glistened like a placid lake. The multihued summer wear of the passengers, contrasted with the whiteness of the ship, made the decks a place of animated colour. The swimming pool soon became the most popular place for young people, while the less energetic sat in the deck chairs reading, talking or simply staring out to sea. Others visited the coffee bars and other shops aboard the ship.

The ship was an easy place to witness for Christ. The majority of the passengers wanted to talk and make friends among the many nationalities on board. Being aboard the same ship created a sense of camaraderie which made conversation very easy. I quickly made friends with two Malaysians, an Indian and a Filipino. All I spoke to showed a keen interest in my testimony and graciously accepted the Christian literature I offered them.

The journey took five weeks. Our first port of call was Port Said in Egypt where we were advised not to leave the ship because of political trouble ashore. Because of this a host of local traders were allowed on board the ship to sell their wares. The decks were soon transformed into an eastern market place as dark-skinned traders set up their stalls and began to compete for the attention of the passengers. Beautiful silks, shining copper and brass ware, leather goods and silver jewellery were very popular among the passengers who went from stall to stall comparing prices and haggling with the merchants. The ship's officers were on hand to give advice on price and quality, ensuring that no passengers were really 'fleeced'. One or two traders brought on board intricately carved wooden chests and other furniture, whilst yet another tried to sell curved swords with jewel encrusted handles and scabbards. Even for those who did not intend to buy anything it was a fascinating diversion.

Those traders who were not fortunate enough to be allowed on board the liner took to small boats and began to encircle the huge ship. They held aloft their wares and shouted out prices which undercut those of the traders on board. From their little boats laden with silks and leather ware they threw up lines with great accuracy into the hands of passengers. Passengers hauled up a basket at the end of the line. Into the basket they placed their money and then lowered the basket down the side of the ship. The trader then put the purchased article in the basket and the passenger pulled it up again. The basket was then passed on to the next interested customer. To me it looked a pretty risky way to make a purchase, but it was certainly fun to watch. Our next port of call was Bombay. We stayed there for three days. A great variety of bus trips and guided tours were arranged for the passengers who queued enthusiastically to make their reservations. These tours did not appeal to me. I chose to walk the streets of the sprawling city. It was an experience I shall never forget. I travelled light, wearing just shorts and shirt. I left my watch and most of my money on the ship. I just walked and walked. Once out of the dock area I kept to the main road. After walking for about a mile I turned into a narrow road that led away from the shops and business buildings. I soon got used to the noise and heat. The roadside barbers, the small market places, and the bright saris worn by the women fascinated me.

What shocked and alarmed me was the utter poverty of some of the people. As I walked and walked I would often wander down back streets. Whole families lived by the roadside in makeshift shelters of cardboard boxes. They seemed to me to be clustered together in unnecessary proximity until I realised that each makeshift dwelling was built as close to the public toilet as it could get. Naked children gathered around me asking for money. Beggars slept on the pavements. I had never seen such widespread poverty close at hand before. It disturbed me greatly.

Before I set out the second day I filled my pockets with chocolate for the children. I struggled with a sense of shame that I could do so little. To those who slept by the roadside in the sprawling city the magnificent P. & O. liner must have appeared as a floating palace, a different world. As for me, our council flat in Deptford took on a new perspective. I realised that we were among the rich of this world.

On the afternoon of the third day I abandoned my walking. I went to a swimming pool administered by expatriates living in Bombay. It was a beautiful place with gently undulating lawns spotted with wide-leaved palm trees to shade visitors from the burning  sun. It was a great contrast to what I knew lay on the other side of the high walls which secluded this place from the surrounding city, but I could understand why such a place had been built by those whose occupations demanded that they and their families spend long periods in such a city. In a sense it was like the ship I travelled in, a different world.

The lush greenery of Sri Lanka, or Ceylon as it was then called, was in stark contrast to the brown, dusty streets of Bombay. We docked there on a Saturday and were given two days to visit the island. I accompanied one of our Bible study group to visit a missionary friend who worked with the Brethren Assemblies in the suburbs of one of the larger towns. The missionary's home was spacious, cool and bright. The light-grained wooden floors were highly polished. The rattan furniture was very comfortable. All was plain and simple.

The meeting hall was a wooden building, almost square in shape. It had long open windows, screened to keep out any troublesome insects. From the ceiling hung four large, propeller-shaped fans which revolved lazily creating a pleasant breeze upon all who assembled. We were given a warm welcome. When the service was over people stayed behind to sit and talk with their friends. There was no sense of rush or hurry. One was left with the sense of peace and quietness which for the most part had pervaded the meeting itself. It was as if the fans revolving slowly and silently above had somehow influenced the people congregated beneath them. I enjoyed being there. It was the first service I had ever attended in a land other than Britain.

In Singapore I attended a church in an office block. The large room was packed full of enthusiastic young people. They sang many lively choruses and enjoyed expressing themselves in worship by using all manner of musical instruments.

In Manila, the capital of the Philippine Islands, I visited the Christian Literature Crusade print shop. I had my instructions how to reach the print shop from the quayside. They were written on a piece of paper I had brought with me. I simply gave the piece of paper to the driver of the first taxi I could find and sat back to enjoy the ride. It was the most hair-raising car ride I had ever experienced.

The driver spoke English. Once I was settled in the car he promptly instructed me to hold on to the door handle, especially when we went round corners, because the door sometimes opened! He then set off at breakneck speed. When we got to the city he weaved in and out the traffic as if in a race. I tried to enjoy all that I saw from the taxi, but had to concentrate on holding the door handle. All I can now recall are the colourful jeepnies which seemed intent on beating us to every corner. The car lurched first to the right and then to the left. After we had rounded one corner at great speed the driver stopped the car. He then got out and went to the back of the car. Thinking we had arrived at our destination I got out too. I tried to pay my fare, but the driver explained that we had not yet reached the address written on the piece of paper. He had stopped to make "an adjustment to the car". He then got me to help him realign the body of the car with the chassis. He nonchalantly told me that it "drifted a bit"!

In Hong Kong I went with a fellow missionary to visit the high-rise buildings where a friend of his was doing evangelistic work. We went inside a flat which was vacant. It consisted of two very small bare rooms. The concrete walls were not plastered. Apart from the electric lights, electricity sockets in the walls and a water tap, there were no other amenities. My friend explained that very few people cooked meals in their flats, but purchased them already cooked from vendors and small shops. They brought these meals home to eat. Again my mind turned to the council flats in Deptford. We had been living in luxury but did not know it!

While in Hong Kong I travelled by train to the border with mainland China. I gazed into China and tried to imagine what it would be like to be a missionary there.

In comparison to what I often saw ashore, the liner was indeed a floating palace. The meals were sumptuous, the cabins comfortable and the amenities excellent. In order to make friends among the passengers I took part in many of the sports and competitions organised by the ship's staff. I did well in the swimming and table tennis, and was the surprise winner of the greasy pole contest which took place during the 'crossing the line' festivities. Through these activities I was able to share my faith with many of the young men on board.

For the latter half of the journey I was asked by the other Christian passengers to lead the evening Bible studies. This in turn led to the opportunity to hold a service in the ship's ballroom one Sunday afternoon for any who wished to come. As the time for the service approached, people began to stream into the ballroom. Many of those who had become my friends through the sporting activities came to hear what I had to say. By the time the service was due to begin some 400 passengers had gathered. Among the sea of faces were Indians, Europeans, Malaysians and Filipinos. I spoke from Isaiah 53 and gave a straightforward gospel message. At the close of the service many came forward to receive Gospel portions and booklets. I was greatly encouraged. I felt my life as a missionary had really begun in earnest!

After five weeks at sea we finally came within sight of the coast of Japan. By this time I was impatient to get there. We stopped first at the port of Kobe, then sailed up the coast to my port of disembarkation, Yokohama. As the huge liner slipped quietly into its berth I began to panic. Hundreds of people lined the quayside waving excitedly to the passengers they had come to meet. Passengers waved back and shouted as they recognised friends and family. I wanted to wave and shout, too, but I had no idea what any of the Christian Literature Crusade workers looked like. I doubted that anyone would recognise me among the crowds. I raced downstairs to my cabin and on the biggest piece of paper I could find wrote just three letters, CLC. Back on deck I waved it to and fro until a small group on the quayside began to wave in my direction. With a deep sense of relief and thankfulness I realised that I had finally arrived in Japan.

My new colleagues from CLC Japan soon had me comfortably seated in their car and on my way to the mission headquarters in the suburbs of Tokyo. For the next three years Tokyo was to be my home.

## Chapter Five
# THE LION AT THE GATE

"An invention of the devil to hinder the spread of the gospel!" was how the early Jesuit missionaries in the mid-sixteenth century described the Japanese language. Though experienced travellers and linguists, they were bewildered by it. The modern missionary, even with all the latest language aids available, shares the same bewilderment.

The leader of the early Roman Catholic missions to Japan, Francis Xavier, also wrote, "Now we are like so many statues among them, for they speak to us about many things whilst we, not understanding, hold our peace. And now we have to be like little children learning the language." Although separated by over 400 years, I felt exactly the same as he!

The Japanese language has also been described as 'the lion at the gate', alluding to the statues of twin lions that stand guarding the entrance to many Buddhist temples. One cannot gaze upon the temple treasures unless one first passes the lion at the gate. The Japanese language guards the treasure house of Japanese culture. The culture cannot be truly appreciated unless the 'lion at the gate' is slain. The language must be mastered, even if in the process it is murdered first! This being so, it was perhaps appropriate that I began my formal language study in the basement of a Buddhist temple.

The Temple of the Golden Land stands in a secluded copse of ancient pine trees just over the road from the Tokyo Tower, the tallest metal structure in the world. (When it was built the Japanese made sure it topped the Eiffel Tower by a few feet.) The Temple of the Golden Land is neither large nor famous. Thousands of tourists have either walked or driven past it on their way to the famous tower without giving it a second glance. While tourists and Japanese alike queued at the foot of the tower in order to ride the elevator to the top and thus gain a spectacular panoramic view of the great city, I descended a little flight of stone steps which led down to the basement of the secluded temple.

The language school was very small. In fact, it was unlike a school at all. The grounds of the temple were well tended. A gravel path led through an ancient wooden gate which formed the entrance to a small but pleasant garden of carefully manicured pines and shrubs. Just to one side of the main temple building the path branched off and led to the small flight of stone steps, which in turn led to the entrance to the language school. The door at the bottom of the steps opened into a room the size of a medium lounge. From the ceiling was suspended an ancient iron kettle which hung directly over a charcoal burner set in a low, highly polished table. The table was surrounded by comfortable easy chairs. The room had a strong Japanese flavour but also put the newcomer at ease. It was a masterful blend of ancient Japan and modern comfort.

To the left of the entrance was a small office from which the principal of the school emerged to greet me and interview me as a prospective student at his school.

He introduced himself as Mr Nitoguri. Nitoguri is an unusual name in Japan. It translates directly into English as 'Mr Second-class Chestnut'! Mr Nitoguri was a tall, slim, smartly-dressed, efficient-looking middle-aged Japanese gentleman.

With a series of polite bows and hand gestures, his face aglow with welcoming smiles, he soon put me at ease and invited me into his office. In excellent English he began to interview me. After inquiring about my academic record, or lack of one, he then asked me why I had come to Japan, how long I intended to stay, what I hoped to do and whether I intended to read and write Japanese as well as speak it.

I, in turn, informed him that I intended to be in Japan for many years and that I desired to speak, read and write the language. I also assured him that I intended to study hard. He then announced that I could commence attending the school from the following week.

Going to this particular school was something in the nature of an experiment. No CLC missionary had ever studied there. I was to be a 'guinea pig'. I soon discovered why it was such a small school. There were no classes! The teaching was all personal tuition. Mr Nitoguri explained that the school would tailor-make a course for me. All students had their own unique courses. My course would be based upon the information I had given him at the interview in his office. No text books would be used.

What an efficient system it was! A teacher was assigned to me, a young lady of impeccable manners. She was always smartly dressed, always cheerful, and always enthusiastic. She was also a strict disciplinarian. She was my teacher for eighty per cent of the time I spent at school, and was directly responsible to Mr Nitoguri for my progress in the language. Four days a week she handed me specially-graded and appropriately-selected printed sheets of handwritten Japanese script. I was expected to understand, read and even commit to memory these sheets of script by the following day, when she would go over any problems I had encountered. How she made me work! She was highly motivated, highly efficient and highly effective. She had the uncanny knack of pushing me to my limits without causing me to despair.

My life virtually revolved around those printed sheets of Japanese script. The journey to and from the CLC headquarters was a long and arduous one. It involved a car or bus ride to the local station, a train ride to a large, central, commuter terminus, an underground train across the centre of Tokyo and then a ten-minute walk to the school. The trains were often packed to capacity, but I endeavoured to use the travelling time for the memorisation of the printed sheets of Japanese script. At times the trains were so crowded it was impossible to turn over the page. At each station, and as I walked from the last station to the school, I constantly studied the advertising hoardings to see if I could recognise any of the Chinese characters as being the same as those on my printed script. I travelled the same route every day. I was determined not to get used to seeing the same Chinese characters day after day without knowing what they meant. I had learned at the Wycliffe linguistics course that one of the chief assets in language acquisition is a consistent sense of curiosity.

Each evening after school I would spread my printed sheets on my bed, surround them with dictionaries and grammars, kneel on the soft traditional matted floor and set about the task of comprehension and memorisation in preparation for the classes the following day.

One night I fell asleep on my knees. I awoke at around four o'clock in the morning with sore knees and a great sense of disappointment. While asleep I had dreamt I had experienced an Acts 2 miracle and could now read the Japanese newspaper! I climbed into bed realising that to master the memorisation of the 2,000 basic Chinese characters and their various Japanese readings was going to take a miracle of patience and persistence. A long road lay ahead of me.

I met only one other missionary at the school in the temple basement. All the other students were either diplomats, scholars, businessmen or journalists. It was the kind of situation which normally would have brought back all my feelings of inferiority but it did not. We were like children together. After weeks, even months, of intensive study they, too, could hardly discuss the weather. Everyone found even the simplest conversation in Japanese very difficult. Compared to many of my fellow students, who had to learn the language while engaged in a profession, or within the confines of a fixed number of months or years, I had many advantages. I was young, highly motivated, single, and I had long years of life ahead of me in Japan.

I grew to appreciate the school in the temple basement. I owe it a great deal. I spent three years as a student there. I attended eight hours a week for the first year, four for the second and two for the third. Before the end of the second year I had been asked to preach in Japanese at the local Baptist church.

However, not even the finest language school can save the language student from the many embarrassing mistakes and resulting culture shock which functional illiteracy produces.

My first embarrassing moment was a result of my own zeal to begin language study. I was determined that my first Sunday in Japan would be spent in a Japanese church. Many of the missionaries, for the sake of their children, worshipped and fellowshipped in English-speaking congregations on American military camps in and around Tokyo. It was easy for me, being single, to choose to worship at the nearest evangelical Japanese church.

The Japanese young people at the CLC headquarters offered to take me to the local Baptist church, but warned me that I would need to introduce myself in Japanese to the congregation at the conclusion of the service. This, I was told, was the Japanese custom. One of the young CLC workers offered to teach me the appropriate sentences. I immediately remembered one of the language learning techniques I had been taught at the Wycliffe course, the tape loop. I made a loop of recording tape, filled in the spools on my tape recorder so that the same piece of tape revolved constantly. On to this loop of tape one of the Japanese young people recorded the sentences for me.

"Watashi wa McElligott Patrick desu. Igirisu kara mairimashita. Yoroshiku onegaishimasu". ("My name is Patrick McElligott. I have come from England. I am glad to make your acquaintance.")

The sentence filled just half the tape loop, the rest was blank. This gave me the time to repeat the sentences every time the tape went round. I played the sentences over and over again, mimicking them constantly trying to copy them exactly. By the time Sunday arrived I could say the sentences without even thinking.

I sat through the service without understanding one word. At the appropriate moment after the service my friend nudged me to stand up and give my self-introduction in Japanese. The words just rolled off my tongue. I sat down very pleased with myself! Almost immediately the church young people surrounded me and bombarded me with all manner of questions. They did not realise that I had just expended my complete Japanese vocabulary. I had not really understood what I had said, let alone what they were saying. I felt a complete idiot!

A few weeks later I decided to get used to driving in Tokyo. As a literature missionary I knew I would be expected to master driving in Japan. I thought, the sooner the better. I took out an old CLC van, which was used for local transport and book deliveries. I intended to keep to the local streets around the residential area in which the CLC headquarters was located. It was a bright sunny day but I did not dare to try to enjoy the scenery. The streets were very narrow. There were no pavements. Open drainage channels just over the width of a car wheel bordered each side of the road. I took great care. I found a wider road and drove down it.

The further I drove the greater the number of pedestrians there seemed to be. I was concentrating on not hitting anyone when I became aware that a left turn had brought me into a very busy, crowded shopping street. It was a place of much movement and abundant colour. Red, blue and gold streamers suspended across the street fluttered in the breeze. Plastic, pink, artificial cherry blossoms had been tied to the lampposts by the shopkeepers. Loud music from the shops gave the street a kind of carnival atmosphere. Hundreds of shoppers milled around, spilling out on to the road from the shops on either side. The road became narrower and, consequently, more crowded. I concentrated hard on my driving. I did not want to mark the end of my first month in Japan with a traffic accident!

Suddenly the shrill sharp blast of a whistle blown to full capacity sounded above the general noise and canned music from the shops. There emerged, seemingly from nowhere, a uniformed man running in my direction. His face, reddened by the effort put into blowing his whistle, was a mask of urgency. He ran forward, his whistle between his teeth. He was a policeman.

My first thought was that someone had robbed a bank or something. His abrupt appearance and the noise from his whistle had an electrifying effect upon the crowds. I looked behind me to see what the trouble was.

The policeman seemed to be heading in that direction. People stopped and began to stare, but not behind me, straight at me!

The excited, red-faced policeman stopped directly in front of the van, refusing to let me proceed. Panic overcame me. I was the culprit, the cause of all this commotion. The crowd gathered round the van as the policeman shouted angrily in my direction, his arms waving frantically. I could not understand a word.

I opened the window of the van. The policeman glared in at me. Only then did he realise he was shouting at a foreigner. His face was transformed into a mask of perplexity. His lips still moved but no sound came out. His face, still reddened by the effort of over-enthusiastically blowing his whistle, appeared to me like some huge noiseless goldfish. I could feel the embarrassment creeping up my neck and spreading all over my face. All eyes turned upon me. The crowd gathered closer. Faced with a foreigner who obviously could speak no Japanese the policeman now knew he had to speak in English. The crowd were obviously keen to see how he would handle the situation. He was well able to cope. He took a firm stance in front of the van, placed his hands on the bonnet as if to push and then shouted at the top of his voice, "Stoppu stoppu! Backu, backu!"

He then pointed in the direction from which I had come. I reversed slowly now purple with embarrassment. I had driven the wrong way up a oneway street. The novelty of the sounds and colour combined with my concern not to hit anyone had resulted in my failing to notice the no-entry sign at the beginning of the street.

Once free from the crowds I drove straight home, went immediately to my little room and flopped onto the bed. I was nervously exhausted. I felt I never wanted to go down that street again. I was in shock, culture shock!

Shortly after this I made my first solo attempt to purchase something in a local shop. I did not go by choice, I was sent.

At the CLC headquarters lived six or seven single members. I was the only non-Japanese among them at most meal times. An elderly Japanese lady, known to everyone as obaasan (honourable grandmother), prepared our meals and looked after us in many other helpful ways. She was like a mother to us. Her traditional Japanese dress, quiet humour, and gentle manner were a welcome contrast to life in the city with its hectic pace and Western trappings. Obaasan spoke no English whatsoever.

One morning I arrived first for breakfast. It was to be toast that morning, but there was no bread in the house. Obaasan wanted me to go and buy a loaf. With her complete lack of English, and my virtually non-existent Japanese, communication was reduced to sign language.

She pointed to the toaster and shook her head. She made a square shape with her hands, cut the air with the edge of one hand and then shook her head again. It took me a little while to understand what she wanted, but at last I got it. She wanted an uncut square loaf. She was a very economical lady and had decided she could get more slices from an uncut loaf than from a presliced one!

When she realised that I understood she produced a coin, placed it in my hand and then slowly enunciated the appropriate Japanese sentence, "Kitte nai pan ikko kudasai." ("One un-sliced loaf, please.") I repeated the sentence to her once or twice, she beamed a smile of approval and sent me off in the direction of the local bakers. The shop was a short walk away so I used the time to repeat the sentence to myself over and over again. I felt good I was actually going to do something useful in the Japanese language. I practised furiously. The baker would surely be impressed with my fluency. I congratulated myself on my ability to say the sentence with ever increasing speed. I was convinced that the local baker would consider me something of a linguistic marvel.

I was blissfully unaware, however, that my zeal for speed of utterance had resulted in a slight phonetic change in the sentence. I strode into the shop, produced my coin and pronounced with an air of nonchalance, "Kitanai pan ikko kudasai."

To my surprise the baker did not seem to understand. In fact he looked quite bewildered. He just stood there. He made no reply. In my confusion I committed a very common 'linguistic' error, "If at first you are not understood, shout louder!"

With no other linguistic resources at my disposal I simply repeated the sentence with increased volume"Kitanai pan ikko kudasai."

The result was simply more confusion and embarrassment The change from kitte nai to kitanai results in a change of meaning . Instead of asking for an uncut loaf I was asking for a dirty loaf. I was demanding, in a loud voice, unclean bread!

The baker eventually realised what I wanted in spite of my ridiculous request. Unaware of my linguistic error I went home to find everyone waiting for me and for their breakfast. When asked why I had taken so long I told one of them who spoke good English that the baker could not understand my Japanese. She asked me to repeat what I had said to the baker. When I did so everyone burst into hoots of laughter. They then explained to me what I had been asking for at the shop.

I could not bear to pass that shop again for weeks. I was quite convinced that the baker had told all his customers about the ridiculous foreigner who wanted to buy dirty bread. When I met people in the neighbourhood my mind was filled with the idea that they had heard the story from the baker and were having a quiet laugh at my expense. In some cases I was probably right! I remembered something else I had learned at the Wycliffe course, "learn to laugh at yourself when you make amusing mistakes. You might just as well, because everyone else will!"

This kind of embarrassment caused by functional illiteracy can result in unreasonable reactions to mistakes of any kind. Without the ability to read, write, converse or understand, the ability to interpret the innumerable cultural clues that surround us in society is lost. Everyday activities, which we would normally accomplish without thinking in our own country, become a constant source of emotional and nervous strain.

Even travelling on a train can result in behaviour bordering on the paranoid. After travelling from the suburbs to the centre of Tokyo with a senior missionary for a few times, I was asked to attempt the return journey alone. My colleague was working late.

The journey itself was quite straightforward. It involved a short walk to the underground station, a fifteen-minute tube ride across Tokyo, change to a suburban line at a large terminus, ride a local train for twenty-five minutes, and finally a bus ride home from the local station. From the busy terminus to our local station there were three kinds of train, express, semi-express and slow. My colleague assured me that they all stopped at our station so any one would do.

I arrived at the busy station just as a train was about to pull out. I jumped on it just as the automatic doors closed. I was pleased with myself. After stopping at a few stations the train went down a branch line my colleague had failed to mention. Soon the train reached the end of the branch line at a station with a strange sounding name,

Toshimaen. Everyone else left the train leaving me in splendid isolation. The train was obviously not going anywhere for the time being because the cleaning ladies came aboard to clear up any rubbish left by the passengers. I felt conspicuous and ridiculous. I was sure the cleaning ladies were having a quiet laugh at me. I got off the train trying to look as if I knew what I was doing. I entered the station toilet, it was the only place to hide from the cleaning ladies! I hid there for a few minutes waiting for them to leave the train. After they had left, and one or two passengers boarded the train, I emerged and got on the train again. In a few minutes the train was on its way back to the main line. I tried to look relaxed but somehow felt that the other passengers had guessed that I was stupid. The train rejoined the main line and stopped at a station I recognised. As it did so another train pulled in at the opposite platform. I rushed across the footbridge and squeezed through the sliding doors just as they closed. I was on my way home again, or so I thought. This train too headed down the branch line. Only one in ten trains went down the branch line. I had boarded two in succession.

We reached the end of the branch line again. There were the same cleaning ladies. I felt sure they would recognise me. I felt pathetic. I mingled with the crowds as they left the train and dodged into the station toilet again, hoping the cleaning ladies had not seen me. I was sure they had. I imagined they they were probably doubled up laughing at this pathetic foreigner by now. Once sure that they had gone I boarded the train again. When we got to the mainline station I followed a passenger who alighted from the train at the same time. In this way I could be sure I would not end up at the end of the branch line once again. I simply could not face those cleaning ladies for a third time! I arrived home nervously exhausted. Everyone wanted to know why I was so late. They had worried about me. I sheepishly told them of my adventures. They tried to encourage me, but I felt as helpless as a little child. I was learning the hard way, but my resolve to master the language was strengthened.

How important it is that Christians pray for first time missionaries going through culture shock. How important it is, too, that more experienced missionaries try to understand the newcomer and his problems. A succession of embarrassing incidents can make a new missionary become very insular as he seeks to protect himself from any situation which makes him feel his own inadequacy and foreignness. For the sake of linguistic progress and future usefulness the last thing a new missionary needs is to give in to the temptation to isolate himself from everyday society.

"What food do you miss most?" was a question I had no difficulty answering.

"Fish and chips!" was my immediate reply.

My new Japanese colleagues agreed that all the items necessary to produce the said fish and chips were readily available at the local market. They announced that we would all treat ourselves to this delicacy. They agreed to pay for it. I agreed to cook it. It seemed a good deal to me until I realised that I was expected to actually go and buy the fish. My colleagues, not knowing what kind of fish would be suitable, gave me the money and dropped me off at the local market. The local market was not unlike the Saturday market in Deptford High Street.

Crowds of people bustled around a variety of stalls. Stall holders shouted loudly to welcome customers and advertise their wares. There were no obvious queues.

I quickly found the fishmongers stall. It was surrounded by a crowd of Japanese housewives. I felt out of place. I was the only man there. Ladies glanced at me and smiled sweetly to me and to one another. Others nudged their companions and made sure they did not miss this unusual sight.

The fishmonger was shouting in a loud voice. He seemed to be saying the same thing over and over again. It was not like anything in any of my printed sheets of language study. Housewives answered him and were served with gruff efficiency They paid their money which the fishmonger quickly stuffed into a money pouch at his waist. He gave small change from a wicker basket suspended by a strip of rubber from the roof of the stall.

It seemed to me more like an auction than a market stall. As one after another were served and went on their way I was slowly being projected towards the front of the crowd. Others pressed in behind me. I wanted to run away but it was now impossible. I began to panic. None of the fish on display looked a bit like cod. The names and prices were all in Japanese. I couldn't read a thing. Before long I was at the very front of the crowd. I tried to look intelligent. I stared intently at the fish, trying to give the impression that I knew what I was doing, but was merely undecided. I noticed some fish that looked as if it might be suitable, but how could I order it? As soon as I had plucked up the courage to open my mouth someone else would give their order to the fishmonger and get served. I was never quick enough. I felt increasingly conspicuous and stupid. I did not know what to do. All I could do was stand there!

Finally the fishmonger came to my rescue. He turned his attention toward me. He stopped his shouting and asked me in slow, polite, and simple Japanese, "And what would you like, honourable customer?"

Ladies sniggered to each other. Then all eyes turned towards me. I stood there 'in all my splendour' - a man buying fish, the only man there, and a foreign man at that! Silence descended upon the crowd. "That over there, six bits please," I spluttered out, pointing to what seemed to me to be most like cod.

As the ladies heard my pathetic attempt to speak Japanese they responded by turning to one another and declaring politely; "Doesn't he speak the language so wonderfully well!" the standard reaction to even the poorest attempt by a foreigner to speak Japanese.

I paid my money while the hush continued. The fish was twice as expensive as I had expected. With ever-increasing embarrassment I searched in my pockets for more coins. The transaction completed, I clutched my packet of fish and made my way to the back of the crowd. The noise immediately returned to its previous pitch. The foreigner had been served!

To this day I do not know what kind of fish it was. It certainly was not cod, but it tasted all right plastered with salt and Japanese vinegar. For the most part these embarrassing experiences only served to increase my determination to study the language. I knew that the more I could understand the language the less frequent these incidents would become. There was, however, one incident early on in my missionary life that resulted in abject despair and a strong desire to get the next plane home. It was a relatively unimportant occurrence, but culture shock has the effect of magnifying even the smallest of problems.

Asked to deliver a few boxes of books to a small country church I set out in high spirits. Here was a chance to be really useful! The weather was fine. I had a packed lunch. A journey of just over fifty miles lay ahead of me. It promised to be an enjoyable day as I set off along a major highway towards the countryside. After a drive of about two hours I found the town I was looking for. From then on things went wrong. My attempts at Japanese map reading failed me. I could not find the church. I asked one person after another. Some said they had never seen a church in the town. Others sent me off in different directions. I went round and round the town. Some streets were very, very narrow, and I carefully maneuvered the van along streets and paths I would never have chosen to drive along. All was to no avail. I simply could not find the church. (To this day I still do not know where it is. I was probably looking for a church building with a steeple and a cross on top, whereas many Japanese churches are simply houses with notice boards outside. I might well have gone past the church without recognising it!)

After hours of fruitless searching I concluded that my only course of action was to return home. I imagined how foolish I would appear bringing the books back with me after a journey of over one hundred miles.

On my way back, while passing through a large town, the interior of the van began to get very warm. I began to perspire as the heat increased, yet the dashboard indicator registered normal temperature. Driving along a busy thoroughfare in the town the engine cut out completely. I rolled the van to the side of the road, got out and opened the bonnet to take a look at the engine. Flames leapt out at me! The battery case and wiring was on fire. The battery case was actually melting. I panicked, and rushed into the nearest building, a large insurance company office and shouted, "Fire! Fire! My car is on fire!" Immediately one of the office workers leapt to his feet, took a large fire extinguisher from its case and ran out to the road with me. His subsequent actions confirmed my belief that inherent in almost everybody is the latent desire to have a go with a fire extinguisher. Either that, or this particular man needed to vent his frustrations in some way. Or perhaps he simply did not know how to turn the thing off.

He proceeded to empty the complete contents of the large extinguisher all over the engine of the car. In seconds foam was everywhere. He then promptly disappeared.

I was left hiding in the broken-down van, covered in dirt and sweat. I considered the situation: a broken-down old van, no success all day, unable to read the map or telephone directory, stuck in a town in which I did not know one person, still thirty miles from home, utterly embarrassed and dejected.

In England I would have simply looked up a garage in the telephone directory or contacted the AA, but here I could do neither.

Feeling absolutely useless I heaved a big sigh of despair, rested my head on the steering wheel and began to talk to myself, "What on earth am I doing here, sitting in a broken-down old banger, covered with oily sweat, the laughing stock of passersby, in a strange land halfway round the world from home?"

I was completely discouraged, discouraged to an extent I had never previously experienced. If by a wave of a magic wand I could have been transported to Deptford High Street I would have had no hesitation at all, I would have waved it immediately I was ready to give up.

As I sat there, to my utter surprise, completely unannounced, a breakdown truck pulled up in front of the van and began to prepare to tow it away!

I was about to experience the kindness and efficiency of the Japanese. The reason the young clerk with the fire extinguisher had disappeared so quickly was to return to his desk and phone his own local garage. He had explained the situation to the garage staff and requested help on my behalf. The friendly mechanic who towed me away soon had me cleaned up and sat down in the garage office. While I had a refreshing cup of tea he started to work immediately on the van. Within two hours he had the van cleaned, fitted with a new battery, rewired,

tuned and running perfectly. I returned safely, but still with the books
I started out with.

Though a wasted journey as far as the books were concerned, the day
bore fruit of a different kind. I had learned that the devil is not
so much interested in the relative size of the problem through which
he seeks to cause us despair, but in the depth of discouragement into
which he can cause us to fall. What he had not been able to accomplish
through the difficulties of the language he had almost achieved through
a burnt battery case! It was a valuable lesson for me.

I also learned that, assuming the clerk was not a Christian, the non-
Christian can be just as kind and thoughtful as the Christian. I was
greatly challenged by the clerk's example. He had proved himself to
be a modern 'good Samaritan'. I regret to this day that in my despair
I did not inquire after his name and address.

Other unexpected fruit was forthcoming. The mission-hall fellowship
in Deptford, upon hearing of this incident, saved and worked hard in
order to send sufficient money for us to buy a new vehicle. This we
did. We were never at the mercy of old bangers again.

My best day for language study was Sunday. I attended the local
Japanese church from my very first Sunday in Japan. After my self-
introduction and subsequent discovery by the church young people
that I could not speak a word of Japanese, they did all they could to
help me. I quickly made some friends among them. Because I was
the only foreigner there the young people asked me if I would teach
them English Bible for twenty minutes after the worship service each
Sunday as part of their young people's meeting. I agreed to do so. I
stayed with them for their whole fellowship time.

The pastor of the church seemed very grateful for my cooperation
with the young people and for my regular attendance at the church. It
was a small church with an average Sunday attendance of about
twenty-five people.

My participation in the young people's meeting made it impossible
for me to get back to the CLC headquarters in time for lunch. When
the pastor realised this, he invited me to have lunch with him and his
deacons in the church vestry each Sunday. I gratefully accepted his
invitation.

Each week after the young people's fellowship meeting I joined the pastor and the three or four deacons in the vestry The meal was usually sushi (small rice cakes with raw fish in top). Each week the meal and relaxed fellowship imperceptibly changed into a deacons' meeting. Somewhere along the line the conversation changed from general topics of interest to church finances and future plans. I only became aware of this because of the recognisable documents and figures produced. I could never tell where the lunch finished and the deacons' meeting began. I just remained there with them till everyone else went home. This was normally around four o'clock.

I did this for the whole of my first year. To this day I do not know what they thought of me. Perhaps they considered me some kind of deacon because I was teaching the young people. Perhaps they did not have the heart to tell me to leave. Perhaps because they knew I hardly understood a word they were saying, it did not matter to them whether I stayed or not! However, as a result of this I was hearing a great deal of natural Japanese each week. What with the worship service, the YPF, lunch with the deacons, deacons' meeting, evening service and after church fellowship, I was hearing mature Japanese language for between eight and ten hours every Sunday.

Thankfully the Wycliffe course had taught me how to listen to hours of foreign language with profit, without getting mentally exhausted. Sunday was my most profitable language study day, and it was all free tuition!

On the days I was not at language school I helped at the CLC shop in central Tokyo. Work in the shop was fascinating. Most of the customers were, of course, Japanese. Among them were pastors, evangelists, students, office workers and children. The Japanese section of the CLC was on the ground floor. It opened on to a very busy thoroughfare. A constant stream of people passed the shop from morning until night.

The shop was strategically located at the heart of one of the busiest university areas in the city. It was also very close to the part of Tokyo most famous for its many bookshops. The shop was rarely empty. Many university students needed to obtain Bibles as a text for literature courses at the universities. Opportunities for personal work in the shop were numerous. Lack of language ability was the great barrier to fruitfulness.

Having been born and bred in London, I thought I would soon feel at home in a large city like Tokyo. I soon discovered that Tokyo was very different from London. The crowds were so much greater. Central places like railway and bus stations seemed so much more hectic.

The first time I went to a major railway station in Tokyo and saw the crowds I asked my missionary colleague what special event was taking place that day. He replied, "Today is Saturday. There are not many people about!"

*View of Mount Fuji*

On some stations in Tokyo white-gloved station attendants actually pushed people into the trains, cramming them in, in order to get the sliding door closed and the train off on time.

The constant barrage of loudspeaker announcements in public places, the visual impact of hundreds of Chinese characters in every direction I looked, the pressing crowds and the sheer pace of life, all combined to make the great city a place of bewilderment and confusion to the newcomer.

The first few months passed by. The novelty of life in Japan began to fade. A pattern of life emerged: language school followed by personal study often late into the night; work at the CLC bookshop followed by more language study in the evening; Saturday afternoon for letter writing and shopping, followed by Sunday spent with the fellowship of the local Baptist church. My struggle with 'the lion at the gate' had begun.

Chapter Six
# A CHANGE OF COURSE

---

Sarah arrived in Japan in January 1966. She was immediately dispatched to the city of Kyoto, some 250 miles away There in the ancient capital Sarah studied Japanese, worked in the CLC bookshop, and lived in the flat above the shop premises.

Kyoto is a beautiful city. Among the modern office blocks and hotels are many ancient buildings and much traditional architecture. Because Kyoto is one of the great centres of Japanese culture, and because it hosts no industry of any great size or military importance, it was left untouched during the bombing of Japan which took place at the climax of the Second World War. Kyoto is very popular with tourists. Most foreign visitors to Japan travel to Kyoto soon after their arrival.

I, too, would have liked to visit Kyoto but not to see the ancient buildings! It was not possible. Language learning was top priority for both Sarah and me. For the next two years we rarely met apart from the twice-yearly mission meetings which took place at the CLC headquarters in Tokyo. By the time we were married in 1968 we had been engaged for four years, yet had hardly met for three of them. Consequently we had accumulated a number of boxes full of old letters!

When Sarah had completed her two years of language study in Kyoto we were married, in January 1968, exactly two years from the day that Sarah had arrived in Japan. It was a simple ceremony in the Baptist Church I had attended from my first Sunday After a brief honeymoon in the mountains in the middle of winter we began our ministry with CLC Japan in earnest.

*Patrick and Sarah in Tokyo 1968*

We were sent to the city of Okayama, a provincial capital in the southwest of the main island, Honshu. Okayama county is one of the most productive fruit-growing areas of Japan. Grapes and peaches from Okayama are popular all over the country. Okayama city reflected its rural surroundings, the pace of life being so much slower than in Tokyo. People were more cheerful and friendly. They had more time for each other.

The city itself had very few tall buildings. Tram cars still ran on steel tracks embedded in the middle of the main thoroughfares. Like most Japanese cities Okayama had many Western-style buildings, but they tended to be drab, concrete, square blocks. There was little of the shining sophistication seen in the modern architecture of central Tokyo.

This was reflected in the local signwriters' attempts to use English in their work. Mistakes were many. Our favourite example of the inexact use of English was at our local supermarket. The way out was correctly marked as the 'EXIT', but over the entrance was an illuminated sign declaring it to be the 'INCOME'. Considering the price of foodstuffs in Japan perhaps it was not a mistake after all! To one used to life in Tokyo, Okayama had the atmosphere of a frontier town.

The tiny CLC shop was the only Christian bookshop for hundreds of miles around. It was situated on the ground floor of a rather dilapidated Western-style building. It shared the ground floor of the building with a rundown little restaurant which specialised in curry-rice, and did not sell alcohol. The building was owned by the Japanese equivalent of The Temperance Society. Above the two small shops was a meeting hall which could accommodate about fifty people. It was used by all and sundry, including the Mormons, who rented it from time to time for their outreach meetings.

The CLC shop was badly lit. The wooden shelves were dark and dusty. Much of the stock was very old. The shop was manned by a Japanese Christian housewife. She was full of energy and enthusiasm, but had neither the time nor the training to run the shop well. This was why we were sent to Okayama.

Mrs. Y, our co-worker in Okayama, was a truly cheerful Christian. She was very outspoken, often blunt, even to customers. She was always positive and wholehearted. She welcomed us with open arms, and did all in her power to enable us to settle in quickly and smoothly. With her help we were able to assess the situation quickly and decide what to do. Sarah helped her in the shop and looked after the bookkeeping, while I was responsible for ordering the stock and extending the whole literature operation.

I set up a bookmobile network and arranged joint evangelistic literature outreach with surrounding churches. It was thrilling to be fully involved in the ministry of CLC Japan at last.

Sarah and I lived in a small village just outside the city. Our home was a new house, we were its first occupants. Our next door neighbours were also newlyweds. Our landlady who lived in a large traditional Japanese house just down the lane, doted on us as if we were her own children. She simply could not do enough for us. She did everything in her power to make sure we were comfortable and happy.

The pleasant aroma of the newly-laid tatami grass-matted floor pervaded the whole house. In our tiny, bamboo-fenced garden were some sweetly-scented shrubs. When in bloom their fragrance filled the house. We had two small rooms upstairs, and a kitchen and living room downstairs. All the rooms were traditional Japanese in style, with sliding paper doors, pressed grass-mat flooring, and light wooden ceilings. Though a new house, the toilet was of the old-fashioned non-flush variety. It was pleasantly appointed, but basically just a hole in the floor to squat over. The village did not yet have a sewerage system. All the local toilets were emptied by a suction lorry sent round by the local council. When the suction lorry was at work in the village we had reason to be thankful for the sweet-smelling shrubs!

The bath, too, was very traditional. It consisted of a round, deep, tapered, iron tub. The bather just squatted in the tub which was heated by a gas burner directed at the bottom of the tub. It got very hot very quickly. It was rather like an indoor version of the cartoon pictures one sees from time to time of the traditional missionary being cooked by cannibals. Once we got used to it we discovered it was a pleasant way to take a bath.

In the evenings we would sit or kneel on the soft, grass-matted floor. When we went to bed we took our mattresses from the appropriate cupboard and simply spread them on the floor. Apart from two kitchen chairs, the only other chair we owned was the rocking chair Sarah bought me as a wedding present.

Like most newlyweds we were very happy in our first home. We got on well with our neighbours and enjoyed the quietness of the old-fashioned lane in which our little house was situated. Our landlady visited us from time to time, and not long after we had moved in she invited us to her house for tea.

We entered the spacious entrance to her house, left our shoes there and stepped up into the entrance hall. We were shown into a traditional Japanese room in which there was not a stick of furniture. The screens and paper doors were beautifully decorated. A Chinese scroll hung on the wall in one corner. Sunk into the floor was a small square charcoal-burning pit over which hung an iron kettle suspended from the ceiling.

Our landlady, dressed in a fine kimono, knelt beside the charcoal pit and opened a plain wooden box. Her movements were graceful, unhurried and deliberate. From the box she produced the implements necessary to perform the Japanese tea ceremony: a bamboo whisk, a thin bamboo spoon, a rustic, earthen tea bowl and a square of coloured cloth.

Sarah and I knelt on the cushions provided. We waited and watched in silence. Just before the land lady whisked the green powdered tea in the tea bowl she laid out some little rice dumplings for us to eat with our tea. With the freshly-whisked tea in her hand she slid gracefully across the floor towards us. Bowing politely she offered me the cup first. Holding up the cup with two hands I tried to drink it quietly and gracefully, I then complimented her on the tea, with the appropriate words which we had looked up before we came to the house. For me, the taste of ceremonial green tea took a little getting used to! After Sarah had drunk her cup of tea, the ceremony was over and we returned home. It was our landlady's way of telling us that she was pleased to have us in one of her houses.

On warm Sunday afternoons local children would gather in our little bamboo-fenced garden to listen to Bible stories, illustrated with large teaching cards and colourful pictures. One evening a week Sarah taught the children English in our living room. In this way we endeavoured to get to know our neighbours and sought to witness to them of the love of God.

After being engaged yet separated for four years, it was a great joy for Sarah and me to serve the Lord together.

One of our chief delights was to be out on the road together with the bookmobile. As we got to know more pastors we travelled further and further afield. Trips sometimes lasted three or four days and covered hundreds of miles. Driving through the valleys lined with stepped rice fields and hillside orchards to reach the larger towns, we passed through village after village with no church or Christian witness at all. In fellowship with small local churches in some of the towns and villages we arranged roadside bookstalls from which we distributed and sold much gospel literature, Bibles and New Testaments. It was a great privilege to enjoy the fellowship of pastors, missionaries and young people who often stood with us at the roadside and helped with the distribution. As our fellowship with pastors and missionaries deepened we were invited to stay in their homes and preach in the churches.

We were introduced to evangelistic work in the tiny villages of the western seaboard by missionaries who had spent many years ministering to small groups of Christians and seekers. In the fishing villages, meetings would not commence until ten o'clock at night, when it was cool and all the work was over. The meetings would go on until the early hours of the morning. In some of these villages there would be just one Christian. In such cases any Christian visitor would be welcome, even foreign missionaries! Invariably we would receive a welcome second to none!

One church we visited regularly, way out in the countryside, had seen something of a local revival in the past. It was still attended by a congregation of almost one hundred adults. It was a very rare exception. Most rural congregations were very small. We met pastors and missionaries who had given the major part of their lives ministering to less than twenty people each Sunday morning.

We saw at first hand something of the struggle of rural evangelism in Japan. We sought, in some small measure, to take part in the fierce spiritual battle which takes place in areas where Shintoism and Buddhism had held sway without disturbance for centuries. We introduced helpful and inspiring Christian literature to both pastors and congregations, and endeavoured to read as much as possible ourselves, Surrounded each day by books in Japanese, and asked constantly to recommend books related to various topics and problems, further encouraged us to continue a systematic study of the Japanese language. There were no language schools in Okayama. So I wrote to the school in the temple basement. They agreed to use me as a 'guinea pig' in their development of a correspondence course. The work in Okayama quickly began to expand. Literature distribution and sales increased. Opportunities to share our faith from the wayside and from the shop counter abounded. Added to this was the joy of being asked to preach in churches far and wide, while we shared good Christian literature with the congregations. As young missionaries we were greatly encouraged in Okayama. Our cup was full.

After a year of this varied and fruitful ministry, different pastors in the churches we visited began to ask me if I was sure I was in the right ministry. The suggestion was that we should be preaching and commencing new congregations. At first it was easy to dismiss this suggestion. We were perfectly at peace and satisfied with our ministry and fellowship in CLC, but the longer we were in Okayama the stronger became the conviction that I should change the emphasis of my ministry. It was not an easy decision. We were under no illusion as to how difficult the ministry of commencing new congregations in Japan could be. Not only so, Sarah was not at all sure that we should change. However, the longer we continued, the stronger my conviction became. It became so strong that I requested an interview with our field director in order to share my conviction with him.

As a result of this we were moved to Otsu city in Shiga prefecture, the area where WEC International had begun its church-planting work in 1950.

For the last eighteen months of our first term in Japan we were appointed to a dual role. For four days a week we operated a mobile literature work based on the CLC shop in the city of Kyoto, where Sarah had lived for two years while she studied the language. At weekends we assumed the pastoral responsibility for the tiny congregation that the WEC mission had pioneered in the city of Otsu, some forty minutes' drive from Kyoto.

Hemmed in by the mountains to the south, which form a natural barrier between it and the ancient capital Kyoto, Otsu is a long narrow town which stretches for over ten miles along the coast of Lake Biwa,

Japan's largest lake. Otsu began as a small fishing village well over one thousand years ago. It is now a modern city of almost a quarter of a million people.

The steep, wooded mountains to the south of Otsu were the setting for some of Japan's most famous and influential Buddhist temples, temples which were once the headquarters and refuge for thousands of warrior monks who constantly threatened the imperial court in Kyoto during the sixteenth century. Most of these great temples were burned to the ground by Odo Nobunaga (1534-1582), the great unifier of the modern Japanese nation. A few of these temples escaped the conflagration, and to this day Otsu remains a national centre for Buddhism. Otsu is largely conservative in outlook. It is hard ground for the gospel seed.

WEC had worked in Otsu since 1954, yet by 1964 there was still just a handful of Christians. This town was typical of the hardness of the work in Shiga prefecture, where WEC had commenced its evangelistic endeavours in 1950. Geoff and Joan Roberts, experienced missionaries from New Zealand, had pioneered the work in Otsu.

At a time when housing was extremely scarce all over Japan Geoff and Joan searched hard and long to find a dwelling in Otsu. They found an old, formerly-unused, two-storey, wooden-framed, semidetached, small, traditional Japanese house. It needed repairs to the kitchen and bathroom, but once these were undertaken they moved in with their four young children. There were two rooms upstairs, one room, a kitchen and a small entrance hall downstairs. All the rooms with the exception of the kitchen were covered with tatami, the traditional pressed-grass mats which make for flexible use of all the available living space.

Using this house as a base they had seen a small group of people come to Christ. A fellowship had been formed. Among the Christians were a carpenter's wife, a nurse and her two teenage daughters, and a young lady who, after conversion, had gone to Bible School and returned to Otsu as a children's evangelist. There was also an hotel manager and his young daughter, a Christian couple who had moved to Otsu from another town, and a young lady who had been dismissed from her home because of her refusal to deny Christ. (She had moved

in with the Roberts family and slept in the tiny hallway of their house.)
When Geoff and Joan Roberts went on furlough in 1969 Sarah and I
moved into their house and took on the pastoral responsibility for
this small but growing group of Christians. We met each Sunday
morning in the apartment rented by the children's evangelist. The
apartment was very small, if all the Christians came to the Sunday
service they could not all fit into the room. About ten was the
maximum it could hold.

One by one others were added to the group. It became impossible to
continue to meet in the tiny apartment. We prayed much for a more
suitable place. Shortly after we moved to Otsu one of the nurse's
daughters graduated from school and trained as a music teacher. She
needed a room to teach students. Her father extended their house by
building a room for her. It was not used on Sundays so became our
new meeting place.

Our greatest joy in Otsu was to see people come to faith in Christ.
However, we were not always instrumental in their salvation. Working
alongside us was a certain Miss Robinson, a lady who, in my opinion,
stands as a constant challenge to the halfhearted Christian.

Miss Laura Robinson, a retired school teacher from New Zealand,
came to Japan to help teach the Roberts' four young children, who
were all being educated at home. She lived in an apartment just down
the lane from the Roberts' house.

When the Roberts left for furlough most missionaries assumed that
Laura, too, would return to New Zealand. We were wrong. Laura
Robinson stayed put in her apartment in Otsu.

Single, over sixty years of age and unable to speak a word of Japanese,
this indomitable lady developed a fruitful ministry in Otsu by teaching
English Bible to Japanese University students. Hardly a day went by
without young people visiting her flat. In addition to teaching them
English and the Scriptures, she made herself available to them as
both counsellor and friend.

Her door was always open. Her table could always accommodate an
extra student for meals.

She became our co-worker. Her flat was just a short walk away.
Missionaries like Laura Robinson are unusual. She met few of the

requirements that a modern missionary society would expect in their candidates. She lived alone, without the language, but somehow she communicated with her neighbours and was loved by them. Over sixty years old, she began a ministry to Japanese a third her age, but they respected her and sought her counsel. She did her own shopping and travelled around on public transport using English and gesticulation to make herself understood. She slept on the floor, Japanese style, ate Japanese food and drank green tea.

Humanly speaking she was in a situation that would have daunted most young people, even some young missionaries, but she not only coped, she coped triumphantly She led Japanese students to Christ. In spite of her cultural limitations and linguistic handicap she had the two great qualities which far outweighed any other abilities. She loved the Japanese people and was zealous for their salvation. She also had an unwavering confidence in the Word of God. She was a woman of prayer. She had a deep interest in, and concern for, the students who came to her. Their struggles and heartaches became her prayer burden. Sometimes young lady students stayed with her for days. She was like a mother to many of them. They found in her one they could love, trust and respect.

Above all, she was fruitful in her ministry. Christians like Miss Laura Robinson are the salt of the earth. It was a privilege to work with her. She brought all her linguistic problems to us and introduced us to all her student friends. We became a team.

When we first met Mr K, a student at the local Teacher Training College, he was slightly drunk. He had studied hard to get into college but was greatly disillusioned with university life. In his disappointment he had turned to drink. He came to visit Laura, who in turn introduced him to us. We counselled him and tried to help him. A few weeks later Laura persuaded him to go with her to an evangelistic campaign in a nearby city. He came back a child of God. He became a faithful and committed member of the Church in Otsu, graduated from Teacher Training College, and became a very conscientious secondary school teacher. While at the Otsu church he was called into the ministry and is now a pastor in the WEC-related fellowship of churches.

Miss Y. was a quiet, serious, young lady. She, too, was studying to become a teacher. She visited Laura from time to time and began to attend the fellowship in Otsu. We invited her and another student to have a meal with us one Sunday lunch time. After the meal we sat quietly talking about the Christian faith. She began to confess her need of Christ. After being shown some Scripture verses she quietly prayed at the meal table and asked God to forgive her sins and make her a child of His through Christ.

Through many difficulties and some persecution she remained true to the Lord. She grew in the faith. In spite of much opposition from her family she married a young pastor, and now has a pioneer ministry with her husband in one of Japan's neediest regions.

Two other young ladies in the fellowship at Otsu also became pastors' wives.

Miss N who was converted just before we moved to Otsu, became a very gifted children's evangelist, with a ministry much wider than the WEC work in Japan. Otsu church never grew to be a large fellowship, but its contribution to the work of God in Japan has been out of all proportion to its size. Miss Laura Robinson and her ministry was, under God, the catalyst for much blessing and much Christian service in the lives of others.

Otsu was our training ground for our future ministry in Japan. We spent the last eighteen months of our first term there. On most weekdays I was on the road with the CLC bookmobile. Sarah stayed at home looking after our first daughter, Joy, witnessing to our neighbours and fellowshipping with Laura Robinson. Every weekend was spent ministering to the small church in Otsu.

The little group continued to grow. One by one others came to Christ. After outgrowing the little flat we also outgrew the music teacher's room.

When the fellowship heard that the house next door was to become available they decided to rent it. It was very suitable for meetings because the two downstairs rooms were divided by traditional paper screens and could easily be made into one room. Thirty adults could be seated in reasonable comfort. Permission to rent the house was granted. On the very first Sunday after we left for furlough, the fellowship met in their own premises for the first time. The pastor who replaced us lived with his wife in the upstairs rooms. This house became the home of the fellowship in Otsu for the next thirteen years. By the time we arrived home in the UK for furlough, I had been in Japan for six years and Sarah for five. Our daughter, Joy, was by this time almost two years old. The first six years had been a time of learning and preparation for the future. We had experienced the hardness of door-to-door work and open-air preaching, but we had been greatly encouraged through literature and film evangelism. While at Otsu we had the joy of baptising Japanese converts in the local lake. This was a great joy and privilege.

Personal work had been our most fruitful ministry during our first term, by the end of which we were both reasonably fluent in the Japanese language. We had studied hard and long.

We came home to the UK encouraged. Our prayer letter upon our return to the UK expressed our feelings at this time:

*The Church in Otsu in 1970. Miss Laura Robinson in the back row.*

*'It is good to sing praises unto our God'*

*Dear Friends,*

*We come home full of praise and thanks after our first term in Japan. Praise the Lord for supplying all we have needed, and for the joy of sharing in His work in that land of great spiritual need. We come home full of thanks to so many of you who have prayed blessing and strength upon us, and who have striven with us as fellow-labourers for the outreach of vital Christian literature and the building of His church in Japan. We have seen Japanese come to Christ and have had the unspeakable joy of leading some of them to Him.*

*Praise the Lord with us, and pray for us as we seek to share both the triumphs and the trials of our first term, and our hopes and plans for our second.*

*After an initial period of language study Sarah and I were married in Tokyo on 15 January 1968. Shortly after this we moved to Okayama CLC, where our service was one of bookmobile, roadside book stalls, ministry to churches and everyday work in the bookshop. Looking back we praise the Lord for His blessing and protection upon us, especially on the long bookmobile trips. Opportunities were given to preach in many different churches. It was a thrill to be able to minister the gospel even in some non-evangelical churches and to introduce them to vital Christian literature.*

*In the summer of 1969 we moved to Kyoto where our daughter Joy was born. Our work from this time on has been with CLC Kyoto, and with the WEC church in Otsu (pop. 160,000). We then moved from Kyoto to live in Otsu, where we served in a pastoral capacity for 18 months until we came on furlough. Those days, though very busy ones, held many encouragements for us. The CLC shop was completely remodelled in October 1970 and a young couple, Mr. and Mrs. Y, have gradually taken over full responsibility for the shop. We rejoice, too, that a Japanese pastor and his wife have taken over the responsibility of the church in Otsu.*

*We have enjoyed good health, and although we have experienced periods of tiredness, are rejoicing in the fact that 'they that wait upon the Lord shall renew their strength' is not just an encouraging verse of Scripture but a practical reality.*

*We do not know where our new sphere of service will be when we return to Japan. Though primarily engaged in church planting with WEC we still hope to be able to minister through CLC, Kyoto, particularly with the bookmobile work if we are needed.*

*We value your prayers for.*
a       Our return to Japan.
b.      Guidance to our place of service.
c.      Fresh ability in the difficult Japanese language.
d.      Joy's education. She will need to start formal education halfway
        through our second term.
e.      Above all, that we will know the continuous filling of His Spirit.

## Chapter Seven
# BACK TO DEPTFORD

Furlough accommodation is often a problem for missionary families, but on this occasion not for us. The Shaftesbury Society mission hall in Deptford had been without a pastor for some years. The little flat where George and Anna Roberts had lived was empty. It seemed the obvious place to live. It presented us with the opportunity to renew our fellowship with our friends in Deptford.

Deptford had changed dramatically. A four-lane highway now scythed in two the community I had grown up in. Its central barrier, and the fast-flowing traffic, separated the council flats I had known as a boy from the mission hall and its surrounds. Many council flats were badly vandalised. Most ground-floor windows were boarded up to keep out vagrants who would use the flats as temporary dwellings and created a fire risk.

Row upon row of terraced houses where boyhood friends had once lived now stood derelict and empty, waiting to be demolished to make way for new council dwellings.

The Odeon cinema, once the most splendid building in the whole area, had been unused for years. It stood, a ruined shell, with no hint of its former glitter and prosperity. The once brightly-illuminated foyer was now closed off with sheets of corrugated iron which were themselves covered with torn and tattered posters, graffiti and political slogans. Every window was framed with dirty, jagged, broken glass. In the roof great gaping holes had somehow been made. It had simply been left to rot.

It seemed symbolic of the neighbourhood I once knew as home. Most of the shops in the High Street sported steel grills over their windows, as if under siege. Only the pubs remained as they were, seemingly able to survive all and every change!

The sense of community had gone. Change was evident everywhere. Though I had only been away for six years and had received many letters from my friends in Deptford, I was not really prepared for such change. It had an almost physical impact on me. I had, no doubt, built up a sentimental and idealistic picture of Deptford as home during the time away. I should have remembered that the changes had begun even before I left for Japan. I should have been more prepared for what I found in Deptford, but our life in Japan had been too busy to allow us time to ponder what home would be like.

Our friends at the mission hall had been very kind. The three-roomed flat was pleasantly furnished. New carpet had been laid. The kitchen was well stocked with basic foodstuffs. The refrigerator was full.

Once we had unpacked our suitcases and settled in we decided to treat ourselves to a fish and chip supper. I went up the High Street to find my favourite fish and chip shop, and was relieved to find it still standing there. I entered the shop only to discover that the man behind the counter was from Hong Kong! The smiling face that greeted me was oriental. It was the ultimate reverse culture shock!

Change had occurred in the mission-hall, too. With no resident pastor the mission hall buildings were usually empty except when a meeting was actually taking place. Homeless vagrants and other down-and-outs, with their bottles of beer or cheap spirits, used the covered porch of the mission-hall entrance to sit and idle away the hours. We had to pass them to enter the mission-hall yard to get to the door of the flat. Most attempts to help them with offers of good clothing were not usually well received. For the most part they were intent on receiving money alone. Some of them invented all kinds of stories of misfortune in order to gain the means whereby they could buy more drink. For many of them it was difficult to understand the gospel message, for their minds had long since been addled with drink. The yard under our living-room window was at times used by them as a urinal, and for the occasional glue-sniffing session.

We had a constant stream of callers, all of them with hard luck stories, some of them absolutely ingenious. All ended in the same way, a plea for money. A refusal was often met with a string of expletives and the final remonstration, "An' you call yerself a Christian!"

With the occasional stone at the window and firework through the letterbox it took Sarah some courage to answer the door at night if I were not at home. We felt vulnerable and, with nowhere safe for Joy to play, we were grateful to friends who opened their homes to Sarah and Joy while I was away, sometimes for weeks, on tours of meetings telling of the work in Japan. We were especially grateful to a young couple with two children of their own, whose generosity extended to providing us with two weeks' holiday in Cornwall with them. It was one of the highlights of our furlough.

For both Sarah and me to be away from the flat in Deptford presented us with a different problem. While in Scotland visiting Sarah's family, the mission hall and our flat were broken into and burgled. The mission hall lost a good deal of equipment, including a typewriter and film projector. Doors had been smashed in and locks broken. The flat was ransacked and the few small trinkets we possessed had gone.

It was the work of amateurs. The larger items were found displayed in the window of a local second-hand shop just around the corner from the mission hall. The shopkeeper even remembered who had brought the stuff in to sell. He told the police where they lived! The thieves turned out to be members of the mission hall youth club!

Confronted with their crime, they confessed. Two of them received counsel and professed faith in Christ. They began to come to the Sunday gospel meeting but they did not continue for long. It was difficult for them. Change had taken place inside the mission hall, too.

Deptford was now known as inner city. The old, traditional sense of community, for which Deptford had been famous in the past, had now largely disappeared. The crime rate had increased. Vandalism was rife. Those who could move out of the district did so. My own family had moved out while I was in Japan.

These changes affected the churches. Some mission halls had closed, one had become a 'Kingdom Hall'. Most of the churches which remained were depleted in numbers. The Shaftesbury Society mission hall had suffered, too. Boys' Brigade had long since closed down, Covenanter classes had ceased to meet, Sunday school numbers were very low. At the Sunday evening gospel meeting where some sixty met regularly at the time I left for Japan, there were only a dozen or so. Most of those who still attended were discouraged. There was little discipline in the youth club. The work was hard and sometimes dangerous.

Sarah and I agreed to act in a part-time pastoral capacity while on furlough. We did some door-to-door work in the council flats and some pastoral visitation. We were able to help a few families in great practical need by distributing food and blankets, but for the most part it was unrewarding service. I was away from Deptford for long periods on deputation work, sometimes we were away together. Our pastoral and evangelistic work in Deptford was, by and large, spasmodic.

Halfway through our furlough our second daughter, Ruth, was born. I was on a deputation tour in Lancashire and Yorkshire at the time. Because we knew that our second child's birth was imminent, I took Joy with me on the deputation tour. We journeyed from place to place by car, staying in various homes and speaking in many churches. It was a novelty for a missionary to bring a two-year-old on such a long tour. Joy behaved very well. Many Christians who met her on that deputation tour have prayed faithfully for her for the last twenty years. With still two weeks of the tour to go, Ruth was born in London. I hired a good, fast car and sped through the night with Joy curled up on the back seat. We arrived in the early hours of the morning, had a quick breakfast at the mission-hall flat, and then went to the hospital. After we had said 'Hello' to Sarah and Ruth, we sped back up the motorway to Lancashire to take an evening meeting and continue the deputation tour.

What with reverse culture shock, the great changes we saw around us in Deptford, and the distressing circumstances both around and within the mission hall, it would have been easy for us to become depressed at a time when we were supposed to be being refreshed. But we were greatly helped by the practical support and fellowship we received from the small group that remained. We sought, with them, to encourage each other in the Lord.

Some of the leaders at the mission hall asked us to consider staying home to lead the fellowship. There was no denying the need was very great. The Shaftesbury Society mission hall had meant so much to me as a boy and as a young Christian, and still did. It was not easy to leave it and return to Japan. I seriously wondered if my home church would survive. I pondered the possibility of coming home for a second furlough, only to find that my home church, too, had closed down.

We were convinced that we should return to Japan. We were confident that our ministry in Japan had hardly begun. It was no time to consider not returning. Even during furlough I had kept up my study of the Japanese language. At thirty years of age I sat Japanese O level exams, and started to prepare myself for A levels.

In 1972 after one year in Deptford, we flew back to Japan. Joy was three years old, and Ruth a baby of six months. I made the mistake of booking on the cheapest flight we could find. It was certainly a journey to remember! Just before we were due to leave we received our travelling instructions.

Rather than being instructed to go to London's Heathrow Airport, we were told to catch a bus from Kings Cross bus station to Southend Airport, a tiny airstrip on the south coast of England! From Southend we boarded an old ex-RAF Anson to somewhere in Holland. From there we boarded a bus and drove for some hours through the night. Somewhere in Belgium (I think) we boarded a large jet aircraft which carried none of the normal markings of a commercial airline. There was no stewardess service, just coffee and sandwiches all the way to Bangkok, Thailand. There were only about a dozen people on the plane. The front half of the plane was partitioned off but the seating section was so spacious we all had four seats each and could stretch out and go to sleep comfortably.

In Bangkok we were put up in a hotel for the night. We were told to report to the airport at nine the next morning . This we did, only to be told that we could not board the plane because it was full up. We would have to wait for the next one, nine hours later. In 1972 Bangkok

Airport was very primitive. There was no air conditioning . It was very hot and very humid. We had not prepared any food for Ruth. I explained the situation to the airline staff and suddenly seats were found for us!

We have never since travelled the cheapest way!

How grateful we were to see our missionary colleagues waiting for us when we arrived at Osaka International Airport. The unusual journey had exhausted us, but we were back in Japan. Our second term had begun.

I have since met missionaries whose home churches have not simply changed while they have served overseas, but have disappeared completely. Social change in the cities, and the search for employment, has resulted in considerable population shifts. Realignment of Christians from one fellowship to another has greatly increased. The numbers, leadership, strength and resources of churches tend to change far more rapidly these days.

In the midst of all this, furloughing missionaries have to learn to adjust to what, for them, are often traumatic changes. Blessed indeed is the missionary whose home church and personal friends are aware of the difficulties that these changes pose for the missionary and the continuance of overseas ministry!

Chapter Eight
# IN RURAL JAPAN

It was thrilling to be back in Japan again among the fellowship of Japanese pastors and WEC missionaries. From this integrated group we would be sent out into a needy area of Shiga prefecture in Central Japan. Alongside the Japanese pastors, missionaries from USA, Brazil, Australia, Canada, Holland, Germany, Zimbabwe, New Zealand and the UK worked as an integrated team. Being a member of such a multicultural team is itself both a privilege and a challenge. We looked forward to getting back into the ministry of commencing and developing new congregations.

With at least the basics of the language learned, and some degree of cultural awareness attained, we felt that all the time and effort invested in our first six years could now be put to immediate use. Not only so, we were both in good health, our family was growing, the children for the most part were a delight to us, and our fellowship with the Japanese pastors and other missionaries was very encouraging. We felt ready for anything!

We were sent into a rural area of Shiga prefecture called Ritto. Though not an area of any particular natural beauty or great historical significance, Ritto was a pleasant place. The countryside which constituted most of Ritto was typical of much of Japan, a blend of different shades of green: the bright fresh green of growing rice stalks, the lighter shades of the bamboo thickets contrasted against the darker green of pine-clad hillsides. In the older villages and small towns thatched farmhouse roofs were not uncommon, and there were some very ancient Shinto shrines and Buddhist temples.

The motorway between the huge cities of Tokyo and Osaka, completed in the 1960's had really put Ritto on the economic map. One of the major interchanges on this, the busiest of all roads in Japan, had been built at Ritto. This made Ritto a strategic place for transport companies, warehouse and storage firms, and both light and medium industries. To support the influx of new industry, residential housing estates had mushroomed throughout the area. These estates became dormitory towns for the cities of Osaka and Kyoto.

In common with many areas of rural Japan, Ritto had become a mixture of the old and new. Modern factories had sprung up beside ancient farming communities. Whole villages had become surrounded by modern housing estates. Apartment blocks, even high-rise flats, were built beside rice fields. On narrow country roads, for centuries the domain of the farmer's cart, one would often be confronted with enormous lorries transporting hard core to fill in yet more farmland. Or they might be carrying finished electrical goods or motor parts out of rural Ritto and on to the motorway towards the huge consumer market of Osaka, or just further south to the bustling international port of Kobe.

The population of Ritto had climbed to 30,000 by the time we went there. It was a 'divided' population. On the one hand, there were the traditional families strongly tied to the rice fields and the more ancient crafts. In this group religious ties were firmly centred on the local shrines and temples. In contrast, the newcomers were more nomadic. Industrial workers came to Ritto at the bidding of their companies to work in the newly-built factories. Their tenure in Ritto could last between two and twenty years, but was more likely to between five and ten years. These people found their social life outside Ritto at the sports centres, cinemas, restaurants, pinball parlours and bars in the nearest large town or along the highway into Kyoto. For most men in this group Ritto was just a place to work or sleep.

Ritto's modern administrative centre had been erected where rice had been sown and harvested for centuries. The paddy fields had been filled in and a truly magnificent town hall, together with a large community centre, a modern fire station, a secondary school, insurance offices, telephone exchange and banks, had taken their place. There were no large shops or restaurants. At evening time the administrative centre was like a ghost town! Apart from the small WEC work there was no church in Ritto.

We were not the first WEC missionaries to work in Ritto. Soon after they arrived in Japan in 1954, Ken and Doris Sunde from the USA had carried a burden for the area. But it was not until 1963 that they were able to start work there. After much prayer and searching, Ken and Doris purchased a plot of land in an old village community called Ohashi. It was about fifteen minutes' walk away from the administrative centre, and very close to the motorway interchange.

In Ohashi Ken and Doris had built a house using the beams and timbers of a typical Japanese dwelling which had been carefully pulled down elsewhere.

The result was a typical Japanese bungalow with numerous paper-covered partitions and sliding wooden shutters to keep out the rain. It had a large square wooden bathtub big enough for our whole family to get into together, which was heated by a wood-burning stove. The toilet was flushless and was emptied once a month by a suction lorry. The flooring in every room but the kitchen was compressed grass tatami matting.

The house stood in the most traditional of all village settings, right next to the village shrine, the focal point of social and religious life in Ohashi. The shrine stood in an open compound surrounded by stone lanterns and gnarled pine trees. Alongside the old wooden shrine was a dancing platform, a storehouse for festival equipment, and a meeting room for shrine officials and village elders. In one corner of the compound, close to the swings provided for the village children, was a tiled roof which sheltered tiered rows of little Buddhist stone images, before which the village people offered tea and fruit.

Though a Shinto shrine compound, it was not out of place to find the Buddhist images there, for most Japanese do not distinguish sharply between the two religions. They tend to blend into one. Most Japanese are dedicated at a Shinto shrine as a babe in arms. The majority are married by a Shinto priest, but nearly all are buried with a Buddhist ceremony.

In the majority of village homes, in the best room in the house, would stand a huge black-lacquered, Buddhist home-altar, where daily reverence is offered to the family ancestors, and memorial rites performed by the Buddhist priest, while in the kitchen one would find a Shinto god-shelf where prayers for good fortune and safety are offered by family members. The Japanese see no problem in synchronising the two faiths.

The shrine compound was the social and religious focal point of the village. Agricultural working parties, in which all village families were expected to contribute at least one member, gathered regularly at the shrine compound to receive their work allocation for the day. The shrine compound was also used by the village children as a playground. Boys would play baseball, and the girls play skipping and rope games, all in the shadow of the shrine. In the evenings the local women's volleyball team practised there for the annual inter-village tournament.

From time to time individuals would pray before the shrine, or make offerings to the rows of Buddhist idols. There was no set time to do this, but early morning was the most popular hour. Older people would often take their grandchildren with them to teach them to pray and worship.

Ken Sunde purchased his land from Mr A, the head of one of the oldest families in the village. Mr A was a master carpenter by trade, and a village elder. He was a small, wiry, sun-burnt man, both respected and friendly. He had been reluctant to sell the land to Ken because he knew it would be unpopular to have a Christian missionary living next to the village shrine. On the other hand, he was kindly disposed towards Ken and Doris. A compromise was reached. He would sell the land to Ken and Doris if they would promise that no Christian meetings would take place inside the house when it was built. Ken agreed to this, and the building went ahead.

Ohashi is a village with a long history. It is thought that at one time an ancient castle stood there. For hundreds of years it was the home of farmers and craftsmen, but after the Second World War it had become a typical mixture of the old and the new. Of the hundred or so homes in the village there were some long-established families like that of Mr A, who had sold Ken Sunde the land for his house. Among them was a noodle maker, a rice dumpling maker and two other carpenters.

One of the very oldest families was that of the Shinto priest, an official village position which was passed down from generation to generation within the same family The priest held a secular job to support his family, but his house was the village centre for palmistry, divination, fortune telling and all manner of advice and counsel concerning spiritual, physical and social questions. Villagers sought the Shinto priest's advice on such diverse problems as who they should marry, how to be healed from sickness, barrenness in marriage, how to avoid misfortune, and the reasons for misfortune when it occurred.

Among the other village families were an electrician, a builder's merchant, a plumber, a rice biscuit maker, and a small sushi (savoury rice cake) shop. Most of the above families were long-established residents considered native to the village, yet less than thirty yards from the village shrine compound was a large two-storeyed dormitory building which housed single young men employed by the local Caterpillar depot, which had been built close to the motorway interchange. Like most later buildings in the village, it had been built on land which previously yielded rice but which had been sold off by one of the village families.

Our next-door neighbour to the west had moved to Ohashi from Osaka, some sixty miles away in 1950. He confided that he was still treated as an outsider and felt as foreign as we looked!

Once we had rested for a couple of days to recover from the journey back to Japan, we packed our belongings on the back of the mission lorry and moved to the village of Ohashi. Living Japanese style meant that we did not need much furniture. Traditional Japanese houses have plenty of built-in cupboard space so we did not need sideboards, wardrobes or dressing tables. We slept on mattresses on the floor, so did not need beds or bedside cabinets. Apart from the kitchen table and four small chairs we needed no other Western furniture. Our two most treasured pieces of furniture were a small, wooden, foot-pump organ (my wedding present to Sarah) and a rocking chair (Sarah's wedding present to me). Our most valuable possessions were the books we used for study and leisure reading.

All we owned fitted easily on to the back of the small lorry. With our two little girls with us in the cab, we made our way from the mission headquarters in the centre of Shiga county to the little house in the village of Ohashi. The village was to be our home for the next six years.

Ken and Doris Sunde had lived in Ohashi for ten years and had established a good rapport with the village community. We inherited a great deal of good will because of this but we must have been a great disappointment to the villagers.

Our first problem was the garden. Ken was of farming stock, a real 'son of the soil'. His land, which extended on all four sides of the house, was greatly admired by the villagers. Ken had 'green fingers'. He used every available inch of land to produce a magnificent display of fruit and vegetables. He was highly respected for this, because the Japanese themselves are very keen market gardeners. None could compete with Ken. His tomatoes were bigger, his lettuces crisper and his potatoes more abundant. He even grew rhubarb and asparagus, and amazed the locals by successfully growing pineapples, a feat unheard of in that part of Japan.

In contrast to Ken and Doris, Sarah and I came from completely different backgrounds. Sarah had been brought up in tenements in a Scottish ship building town and I in the council flats in London. We knew little about growing anything at all, let alone asparagus and pineapples.

My knowledge of growing vegetables was to witness my mother's annual attempt to grow a few tomatoes from a window box placed on the edge of the back balcony of the flat in Deptford. She rarely succeeded. The trouble was, we did all kinds of odd jobs on the back balcony, like mending shoes, carpentry and cleaning football boots, etcetera. We also stored the coal there. What with one thing and another, the window box got knocked off the parapet and smashed to the ground four storeys below. The tomatoes had little chance of reaching maturity. It's a wonder we never killed anybody with them! There was no way we could keep up Ken's high standards. The villagers must have been aghast to see me try to level Ken's carefully weeded soil in the front of the house and scatter grass seed all over it in an attempt to make some kind of lawn for the children to play on. The kind of grass seed I sowed must have been a special fast-growing variety. Soon after I sowed it I commenced a constant battle to try to keep it down to a respectable length. In the middle of the plot of land in front of the house stood Ken's pride and joy: a fruit-bearing Californian cherry tree. Its leaves afforded shade to the house in summer, its blossom was beautiful and its fruit delicious. Ken had gone to some lengths to import it from the USA.

*The growing family: Ruth 2, Joy 4, Ann 6 months*

We knew nothing about spraying fruit trees. Soon after Ken left, the tree produced a bumper crop of huge hairy caterpillars. It seemed to me that these caterpillars chomped away at the leaves till they were so bloated they could no longer support their own weight. They then fell on anyone under the tree and proceeded to climb up the trunk again. Thus doing, they gave themselves an appetite and began to eat any leaves they had left the first time! Some kind of worm had also burrowed into the trunk of the tree causing it to bleed profusely. I tried to get all the worms out of the trunk by attacking it with a large screwdriver, tracing their presence along the holes they had bored. I got them all in the end, but killed the tree in the process! To the horror of the villagers I chopped the tree down and cut it up for firewood.

Our attempts to grow potatoes, beans and cucumbers on the rest of the land were initially unsuccessful, but Sarah persisted until she had a measure of success.

Ken and Doris had worked hard and long in Ritto. They had done a great deal of door-to-door work in both the older communities and the housing estates. With the help of Miss Yukiko Nakajima, the children's evangelist from Otsu, they had built up a little fellowship and had formed a thriving Sunday school in the house in Ohashi. (The villagers did not mind children's meetings.)

Miss Nakajima was very gifted indeed. Her Bible stories were well illustrated, usually with her own art work, and told in such a way that the dozen or so children who came always listened with rapt attention. She had also commenced a children's class in a nearby village on Saturday afternoons. There, too, the children listened attentively to the Bible stories and the Scripture message. Miss Nakajima loved the children she taught. She played games with them, wrote to them, encouraged them, prayed constantly for them and led many of them to faith in Christ.

Soon after we moved to Ohashi, Miss Nakajima was sent to minister elsewhere. We took on the responsibility for her children's meetings. It was only after she was no longer able to come to Ohashi and the other nearby village that we realised her true worth. We thought the children would lose interest and stop coming when she left, for we could not teach them like she did, but it was not so. For all her gifted speaking, radiant personality and genuine concern for the children, she truly taught them to love Jesus Christ more than they loved and enjoyed her. Even when she could no longer be there the children still gathered with the same enthusiasm. It was a joy to minister after her. It was a great human sadness for us all when she died of a blood ailment when still in her thirties.

The experience of working alongside national Christians who have suffered much for their Master is one of the great privileges of the cross-cultural missionary

Miss Nakajima had her first Bible burned by her parents when she was still a teenager. Her parents forbade her to attend church. Unwilling to renounce her faith, she was confined to the house. All contact with Christians was strictly forbidden, but she maintained fellowship through clandestine telephone calls. Eventually her parents cast her out of the home and disowned her. She went to Geoff and Joan Roberts in Otsu, who took her into their home and cared for her. She slept in the front hall of their house.

From Otsu she went to Bible school, trusting God to supply all she needed. She came through triumphantly. Upon graduation she joined the integrated fellowship of WEC missionaries and Japanese pastors and evangelists, and developed a ministry to young people and children which was owned of the Lord. She became well known far and wide. For most of this time she was disowned by her family.

As her debilitating illness progressed she was constantly in and out of hospital. She was anointed with oil and prayed for, but she was not healed. She developed a ministry in hospital as a personal evangelist. Her love for the lord and those who did not know Him was irrepressible. During her frequent and often very painful treatment in hospital she led men and women to Christ through her loving witness. Under strong medication she was often in distress because of the side effects of the medication she was having but she always had a word of encouragement for others, and a song of praise to the Lord.

We in Britain have much to learn from Christians like Miss Yukiko Nakajima. Her funeral was a great triumph. All her family gathered at the mission headquarters to be there. Her mother had become a Christian. Her father wept for his actions towards her. She typified the motto of C.T. Studd, the founder of WEC International, "If Jesus Christ be God and died for me, then no sacrifice can be too great for me to make for Him."

Miss Nakajima's ministry in Ritto was not confined to children. One of the adults, in whose salvation she played a great part, became one of the first elders in the church at Ritto, a man who later went to Bible school with his wife, and is now in the ministry himself.

Mr M was a successful engineer who worked for a large modern company. He had purchased a house on one of the new housing estates.

His wife was a Christian. She had been converted after her son contracted TB and was treated at a Christian hospital. She had fallen away from the Lord, but had been contacted through Ken's faithful door-to-door work. She began to send her two children to Miss Nakajima's Sunday school. Occasionally she attended the worship service herself. Mr M would often bring the children to Sunday school and wait for them outside in his car. On the way home the children talked about the Bible stories and how they enjoyed them. He decided to wait inside rather than outside and began to listen to the Bible stories himself.

One Sunday morning Miss Nakajima spoke about the One True and Living God who abhorred the worship of idols, and who alone deserved our love and worship. This had a profound effect upon Mr M. He went home and took from the living-room wall a little god-shelf he had made himself to enshrine some sacred articles his mother had given to him. He carried it out to the garden, built a little fire and destroyed it all. He was not yet a Christian but he had 'turned from idols'. Later he was to 'turn to the living God'. Such was the impact of Miss Nakajima's Sunday school lessons.

Evangelism among adults in Ritto had been hard work, the response had not been encouraging. Years of faithful evangelistic endeavour and weekly ministry had not resulted in a viable fellowship being formed. Much seed had been sown and watered, but the harvest had not yet been reaped. There had not been one baptism in Ritto.

Unable to use the house in Ohashi for adult meetings, Ken and Doris had searched constantly for a suitable place for the few Christians to meet. It had not been easy. At one time they met in the storeroom behind a chemist's shop near the administrative centre of Ritto. It was very small. The chemist eventually needed it to store more stock in. They had to leave.

When we came to Ritto, the worship service was held on the top floor of an insurance company office building. Ken had befriended the caretaker. Because the third floor was not being used for anything, the caretaker offered it to Ken on the condition that they did not advertise the meetings in any way, they did not put up any signs at all, and they vacated the building by 12.00 noon.

The room consisted of the whole of the third floor. It was just one big office space. There was no furniture, but we were allowed to use a few folding chairs which we carried to and from the second floor. We met in the middle of this huge room, just three or four of us in a space that could seat a hundred! Until we began to pre-record a few tunes on a portable tape-recorder there was no music to sing by. There was no instrument to play. In the humid heat of the summer, the room was hot and stuffy because the windows had not been opened all week. In the winter we went very early with an Aladdin stove to try to warm the place up before anyone arrived. We huddled round the stove to try to get warm. As soon as the service was over we were obliged to leave.

For the most part only ladies attended. One of these ladies was very faithful. Converted and baptised in another town when she was a young woman, she had married and moved to Ritto with her husband. Come rain or shine, heat wave or downpour, sometimes by bus but more often by train, she journeyed with three young children to the centre of Ritto to be at the worship service. Her husband, although converted and baptised just before they were married, was strong neither physically nor spiritually. He rarely attended.

What with the distance, the children, and her home circumstances she had every excuse for not attending regularly but she was seldom absent. Her faithfulness was, and still is, a model for any Christian. She had within her heart a deep desire to worship God, and a dogged determination to be with other Christians even if they were missionaries.

Much is spoken and written about church growth principles but, in my experience, without Christians like Mrs U. very little would be accomplished in resistant and difficult places.

Mrs U, and others like her, will never know the ministry of encouragement they have had to young discouraged missionaries and pastors serving in hard places. To this day I can recall her cheerful voice calling out, 'Sensei!' (Pastor) as she entered that lonely office carrying one child and leading the other two by hand. Her journey over, she was now ready to praise God. How her presence and word of greeting gladdened our hearts, as Sarah and I, with our own two young children, sat round the Aladdin stove wondering whether anyone would come at all. She would describe herself as just a housewife, "neither wise nor noble", but in the Lord's eyes, and in ours too, she was a treasure.

Another housewife who lived in the same part of Ritto as Mrs U. also attended from time to time. Mrs K. had been converted as a teenager in another part of Japan. Bowing to family pressure she had married a non-Christian. Her life from then on was dominated by her mother-in-law, who ridiculed her Christian faith and forbade her to attend a Christian place of worship. She had fallen away from Christ. Although she had three healthy children, her life was not a happy one. Ken's faithful door-to-door visitation had brought him into contact with her. She attended the worship service under the pretence of going shopping.

Mrs M, the engineer's wife, also attended when she could. These three ladies, together with Sarah and myself, were the basis of the Christian fellowship which met in the insurance office. Each of these ladies had young children. We often had more children at the worship service than adults.

In circumstances like this, every newcomer was a tremendous encouragement. Occasionally an interested person would attend, but rarely twice. The large room was not very inviting. The singing was not very inspiring. A newcomer, not used to Christian hymns and songs, felt ill at ease among so few people. If a newcomer were a man he would feel uncomfortable among the ladies. If the newcomer were a student, he or she would feel uncomfortable among housewives! With no after-church fellowship possible in the room, the prospect of a person attending twice was not great.

Week followed week with no apparent growth at all. Evangelism in such circumstances was difficult. There was always plenty to do, but there was so little fruit. Ken and Doris had seen a few put their faith in Christ, but they had moved away from the area. Like theirs before us, our ministry too seemed likely to be that of seed sowing on hard ground.

Hour after hour of door-to-door visitation resulted in many opportunities to testify to the Lord's love and mercy. For the most part people listened patiently and politely. Many tracts and booklets were distributed to the homes in Ritto. Temples were visited with offers of Bibles and New Testaments for the priests. There was little or no response. We saw no fruit. All this activity did not result in any significant growth in the little fellowship which met each Sunday morning.

*Ruth and Joy McElligott in national dress, just outside the village of Ritto.*

This day-to-day week-to-week evangelistic endeavour was interspersed with special gospel rallies and film shows held in village halls. The hall would be rented, a gifted speaker invited, gospel films ordered, thousands of leaflets distributed, posters displayed in prominent places, and hundreds of homes visited with personal invitations to the meetings.

Many made polite promises to attend. Almost everybody thanked us for our efforts, yet so very few, if any, actually came. Night after night ended in disappointment. It was good to know that we were giving people the opportunity to hear the Good News, but discouraging to have to admit that for all our planning , time, and effort there was so precious little fruit.

Chapter Nine
# THE LORD ADDS TO HIS CHURCH

The pioneer missionary in resistant areas where he is free to witness in whatever way he wishes, faces a constant problem. This problem can be depicted by posing the following question. "What do I do, when all I think I can do I have done, and there is no result?" There are at least three possible answers:

1. Gradually give in to discouragement.
2. Encourage yourself in the Lord. Determine to remain cheerful and faithful. Continue the same activities.
3. Cast yourself upon the Lord. Cry out for His intervention. Believe for miracles.

After just over one year in Ritto my reaction was a mixture of 1 and 3. I was desperate. I cried out for God's intervention.

The passage of Scripture which ministered to my heart more than any other during this time was Acts 16, the account of Paul and Silas at Philippi. Paul and Silas had gone to Philippi to establish a fellowship of Christians. They had seen some initial fruit among the ladies. Lydia and her household had been baptised. From that time on things seemed to go wrong. A young girl was delivered from evil spirits but, as a result, Paul and Silas fell foul of greedy men. They were unfairly treated, unjustly tried, physically abused and finally cast into prison. With their feet held fast in stocks and in considerable pain from the beatings they had received, humanly speaking their position was impossible. Called to see a church commenced in Philippi they now seemed to be captives of their circumstances. They were in pain, darkness and physical bondage. Even so, they refused discouragement. They refused to be defeated. In the most unlikely circumstances for the fulfillment of their ministry they sang praises to God in the dark hours of the night.

I felt in some way our circumstances were similar to those of Paul and Silas. We, too, were called to see a viable fellowship come into being. We, too, had a few ladies attending the fellowship. We, too, were in far from ideal circumstances. We had a far from ideal meeting place. We were surrounded by a resistant people. We were perplexed as to what to do next

We were not in physical bondage, but we were certainly unable to break the spiritual chains which bound those we had come to minister to. I felt we were in danger of becoming captives of our circumstances. Centuries of Shintoism and Buddhism, traditional resistance to change, the conservative outlook in the villages, the economic rat race on the housing estates, the difficulties of the language and the frustration of continual fruitlessness, all added to the apparent hopelessness of our situation. The powers against us seemed to be overwhelming. What could we do? Paul and Silas gave the answer, "Praise!"

We set our minds and hearts to praise God. We cast ourselves upon the Lord. He would have to work on our behalf. We knew the situation was beyond us. In spite of all the difficulties that Paul and Silas faced, the Lord worked on their behalf. By His intervention they were not only freed from their personal bondage, they were enabled to see their basic objective, the commencement of the church in Philippi, achieved in the very place where their difficulties were greatest. In the most unlikely place, the prison itself, the work of salvation took place. The jailor and his family all turned to the Lord and were baptised. The Lord built His church in spite of the opposition and the unfavourable circumstances.

If the Lord could do that for Paul and Silas, could He not do it for us, too? Could He not break our 'fetters' and build His church in Ritto? The answer had to be, "Yes, He could," and "Yes, He would."

Our first major encouragement was the conversion of the engineer

Mr M. The Holy Spirit had been speaking to him. The ministry of Ken and Doris Sunde and Miss Nakajima was now to bear fruit.

He had accompanied his wife to the worship service in the insurance office a few times. He had shown interest. One evening he telephoned me and asked if he could come and see me. His heart was prepared. He quickly confessed his faith in Christ and asked to be baptised. He became a changed man. It was a great joy to baptise him in the lake, in what was the first baptismal service of the church in Ritto. His conversion and subsequent fellowship was a great encouragement to the little group.

The Lord's timing was perfect. Shortly after Mr M. was baptised we were told by the caretaker that we could no longer use the office for our Sunday worship service. This was a blessing in disguise. Mr and Mrs M immediately offered their home as a temporary meeting place for one year.

What a difference it made to have a warm and inviting home in which to meet! We knelt or sat on the tatami floor. We sang to the strains of a small organ. We enjoyed relaxed fellowship after the meeting was over. It was so much easier to invite others to a place that put them at ease. The sense of joy and fellowship in the home of Mr and Mrs M. encouraged us to believe that a church could grow in Ritto.

We learned afresh that the greatest encouragement for a discouraged missionary is to see someone come to Christ. This should always be high on the prayer priority list of those who pray for missionaries in resistant places.

Another encouragement followed quickly. Mrs A was converted. She was a young housewife, not long married. Ken Sunde had befriended her husband through a common interest in tractors. Mr A worked for the local Caterpillar Company. Their first baby had just been born, so I decided to go and pay my respects. Mr A was not yet home from work when I called, but I was invited in to see the newborn baby. Mrs A made a cup of tea, and soon we were engrossed in conversation about the Christian life. She showed great interest and asked many questions. She was eager to know more and more about Christ. She came very close to committing her life to Christ there and then. I left her with the invitation to visit us in Ohashi the following afternoon if she truly wished to become a Christian.

We were thrilled when, the following day, she came to the house in Ohashi. She had carefully thought through the implications of following Christ, and was ready to pray She, too, was truly prepared by the Holy Spirit. She knelt on the floor of the Sunday school room, confessed her sinfulness and received Christ as her Saviour. Tears streamed down her face. She rose from her knees a child of God. Sunday morning worship became a great joy to her. Her conversion was a further encouragement to us all.

These two conversions in particular convinced the little group that things were not impossible. The church could grow The worship service was now permeated with a sense of faith and expectancy. The Christians began to pray for the conversion of their friends and relatives. We prayed much for Mr U. whose wife was so faithful, and for Mr A who declared that he would never become a Christian.

There was certainly a different atmosphere in the worship service. Singing, testifying, sharing, encouraging one another, praying and the preaching of God's Word began to bear fruit. Others joined us, not for the occasional one off visit, but regularly. After nine months in Mr and Mrs M's home it became obvious that we needed a larger place to meet if we were to continue to grow.

Finding suitable premises in Japan is always a problem. Rents are high, land expensive and property scarce. Imagine our excitement when one of our number announced that he had found premises that he thought might be suitable for us to rent as a meeting place.

It was a ground-floor shop close to the administrative centre and the secondary school. It was on the less-populated side of the administrative centre, but new housing was going up all the time. It would not be a sparsely-populated area for long.

The shop itself was completely bereft of any furniture, it was just four walls and a concrete floor. This meant we could model the inside just as we wished. The shop front consisted of six aluminium-framed sliding doors which let in lots of natural light. Even if we partitioned off room for a small office, a creche and a kitchen, there would still be enough room to seat forty people comfortably, and fifty at a squeeze.

The little group of Christians met at the shop premises the following Sunday afternoon to discuss and pray about the possibility of renting the place. It would be a big step of faith for them. The rent alone was as much as the monthly offerings. They would need to pay one year's rent as key money before a contract could be signed. In addition to this, funds would be needed to buy timber and other materials to convert the bare room into a pleasant meeting place.

At this stage of growth in the life of any local church the missionary must take care not to over-influence the group. He should resist the temptation to give too much advice, or allow his personal wishes to be expressed. He must not be the central participant.

A decision was needed quickly, immediately, in fact. The group decided to pray there and then, standing in the middle of the bare floor. I declared that I would go for a walk and pray alone. I told them I would be away for thirty minutes and that when I returned I would abide by their decision. When I got back they were already arranging imaginary chairs and measuring the walls. They had covenanted together to give sufficient to pay for all that was necessary. I believe it was at that moment the Ritto church was truly born.

Anyone who has witnessed the sacrificial giving, the dedication and the enthusiasm of a small group of Christians committed to seeing their own meeting place come into being, will always resist the temptation to allow anyone else to do it for them.

While I worked during the day with one or two others who could give the time, Mr and Mrs M, the engineer and his wife, took over at night, and I helped as a member of his team. We laid a floor, built rooms, fitted doors and made a lectern. The ladies made curtains, fitted out the kitchen and brought utensils from their homes. At weekends the whole fellowship worked together to get the place ready for our first meeting. Never had the set of carpentry tools, given to me as a farewell gift from the mission hall in Deptford, seen so much use! Within weeks we had transformed the bare shop premises into a plain but beautiful place of worship and fellowship. At our thanksgiving service seventy gathered with us from other WEC related churches. It was a very encouraging time, but there was more to come!

"You are the person I have been waiting for!" With these enthusiastic

words of greeting Sarah was welcomed into the local ladies'
hairdresser's shop on one of her rare visits.

"Is the Bible really true?" inquired the hairdresser, a talkative, outgoing
cheerful Japanese housewife of about fifty years of age.

"Yes, the Bible is true. We Christians know it to be the Word of God,"
Sarah answered.

"In that case I had better do something about my life, because I am
not ready for the end of the world!" the hairdresser continued.

Such conversations are very unusual in Japan. Sarah was thrilled at
this opportunity to talk with her hairdresser. She was plied with
questions as the lady did her hair.

The hairdresser had been reading *The Prophecies of Nostradamus,*
which was a best seller in Japan at the time. She had also received a
copy of the book, *The Late Great Planet Earth* by Hal Lindsey, from
a Christian salesman. Jehovah's Witnesses had also called on her, but
she had learned so much from the latter book she immediately doubted
their teachings on the Second Coming of Christ. She wanted to meet
a Christian.

Sarah can still recall with a smile her attempt to use 1 John 1:9 to
teach the hairdresser about God's faithfulness and trustworthiness: *If
we confess our sins, he is faithful and just to forgive us our sins.*

The hairdresser quickly commented, "Well, if He is really God and
He said it, He will do it!"

It was so unusual to meet a Japanese like her in the rural areas. She
was desperate for teaching. She was only free after her shop closed
for the evening, so I had my first Bible study with her in the
hairdressing shop after all the customers had left.

The two of us sat in the empty shop, Bibles opened upon our laps, as
we studied the way of salvation and assurance. Though fifty years of
age she had never opened, let alone read, any of the Bible in her life.
She had never set foot inside a church, but by 9:30 that evening,
amidst the mirrors and hair driers of her shop, she knelt on the floor,
confessed her sinfulness and need of a Saviour, prayed in the name
of Jesus, and thanked God for the cross of Christ. She rose a child of
God. She was a transformed woman.

Her conversion became widely known throughout the village for she had many friends. She had been a great socialiser and was very popular. She conquered her need for strong drink, and constantly spoke of Christ to her friends and customers. She was rejected by many but remained faithful.

We met again the following week for prayer and Bible study. We sat in the shop again, our Bibles opened on our knees. Her prayers were simple and refreshing. She used none of the highly respectful language usually associated with Christian praying in Japan. She had never been to church so she had never heard such prayer. I encouraged her to pray in her own words. She usually began her prayer with the Japanese equivalent of "Good evening , Father, it's me again!" She spoke to the Father as if He were right beside her, which indeed He was! In simple faith she told the Lord how she felt or what she needed. At the end of the second meeting in the shop I asked her about her husband. She replied that she would bring him the following week and introduce him to me.

A week later the two of us sat in the shop once again. After we had read our Bibles for a little while her husband entered. It was immediately obvious that they were like chalk and cheese! She was talkative, full of questions, by nature an extrovert. Her speech was full of idioms and colloquialisms. Her husband was a quiet, reserved Japanese gentleman. Tall, bespectacled and softly spoken, Mr H. had been a devout Buddhist all his life. His speech was measured, scholarly and assured. He showed great respect for the written Word.

He joined us while we continued our Bible study. He sat quietly listening as his wife spoke enthusiastically about her new-found faith and the difference it had made in her life. She told me all the parts of the Bible she had read during the week and plied me with questions about their meaning. Mr. H. listened politely to all the answers I was able to give her. At the end of the Bible study Mr H. with the air of someone seeing the ocean for the first time, simply said, "I never imagined that the real God was so big!"

We closed our time together with prayer. Mrs H. prayed one of her refreshing conversational prayers. In it she included a request that her husband would put his faith in Christ as she had done. After I had prayed I asked Mr H. if he would like to pray too. He replied that he did not yet know the real God well enough to pray to Him, and that he was not sure He really existed.

I asked him if he would like to know for sure. He replied, "Yes."

I then encouraged him to pray during the coming week that, if God really existed, He would give him more light about Himself. We then went home. Because Mr H. was a sincere man I was sure he would pray during the week.

The following Tuesday evening Mr H. came once more with his wife to the shop. Again he listened politely to all that was said. At the end of the Bible study Mr H. accepted the invitation to pray. He simply confessed his sinfulness, gave thanks for the Lord Jesus Christ, and received the grace of God into his life.

I was overjoyed and amazed. Here was a man who for almost sixty years had been a devout Buddhist, a man who had never entered a Christian church and who had never read the Bible, giving his life to Christ upon having heard the gospel message only twice.

I had, in my times of discouragement, begun to believe that such things were hardly possible in Japan.

Their home was transformed. Mr H. broke up and burned the Buddhist home altar that had been his place of worship for most of his life. He had spent many hours praying before it, repeating the same Buddhist chants over and over again until the words blurred and became unintelligible. At such times he had known the experience of falling into a trance and being possessed by the 'snake spirit', as his body swayed slowly from side to side in unison with the ever-repeated chants.

He now had no use for the altar. Though of considerable monetary value, the black-lacquered and gold-leaved piece of furniture was soon a pile of ash in his garden. The altar contained an ancient stone image of the Buddha. It had been in his family for generations. It would not burn. It was difficult to break, and he did not want to bury it in the garden. He took it to the temple he had attended for years.

He told the Buddhist priest there that he had become a Christian and no longer needed it. He tried to persuade the priest to take it. The request was refused. The priest remonstrated with him, telling him that the spirit was still in the image. The priest warned Mr H. that if he did not worship the image while the spirit remained in it some grevious misfortune would befall him.

Not knowing what to do, Mr H came to me for advice. I felt it important that, although he was a very young Christian, he learn to receive his guidance from the Holy Spirit and the Word of God. I pointed out some relevant Scripture to him and sent him away to pray, to find out for himself what the Lord wanted him to do. I was not really prepared for the result.

A few days later he came back with his face beaming. The idol had gone for good. Not only that, Mr H. declared that the church would benefit. I asked him what he had done.

"Oh," he replied, "I prayed, and soon knew what to do. The stone image was very old. I sold it to an antique dealer for a good price!"

Not long after, a sizable gift was found in the church offering box!

Instead of turning his gold into idols, Mr H. had turned his idol into gold! To this day I have my doubts about this method of disposing of idols, but what could I say?

Mr H. has grown in faith and obedience ever since. To the delight of the rest of the fellowship, this couple were added to their number.

Within a few weeks of their conversion their only son began to attend the worship service. He wanted to try to understand his father's new faith. He felt that, being the eldest son, he would be expected to continue his father's faith in the event of his father's death.

He usually sat in the front row by himself a sullen, withdrawn lad of eighteen. A spirit of darkness seemed to hang over him. Although he did not seem to show a spark of interest, after a few weeks he turned up at the church to attend the Saturday night prayer meeting. After the prayer meeting we sat talking in a relaxed, informal way. He showed interest in the gospel, and in a very short time I was enabled to lead him to faith in Christ. We bowed our heads while he prayed a very simple prayer of repentance. Within weeks he was changed into an outgoing, generous, joyful young man. He later became the leader of the Young People's Fellowship for the whole fellowship of churches, married a Christian young lady, and followed in his father's footsteps to become a leader in the church at Ritto.

For those who have never had the privilege of seeing a church grow in a resistant environment, it is difficult to describe how such wonderful and completely unpredictable conversions of the most unlikely people can fill the previously discouraged missionary with hope and joy.

The effect on the fellowship was quite noticeable. Husbands of some of the ladies began to attend, people began to bring their friends, teenagers began to swell the congregation, the creche was sometimes full of little children. Many of the practical hindrances to growth were removed through the suitability of the new premises. We were still a small group, but we were growing.

However, not everything was encouraging. It was during this time of growth and blessing that I encountered my most bitter experience as a missionary. Among those who were beginning to attend regularly was a young family who had moved to Ritto from another church, which was now too far away for them to attend. Although both were baptised Christians, not in fellowship with any other church, they did not feel free to become members of the fellowship which was coming into being at Ritto. Being a small group we were grateful for their attendance and help. In actual fact, it was the husband who had informed us of the shop premises which became our meeting place. Although they had been Christians for years, the husband had spent a great deal of his life at sea on commercial ships. He had begun life ashore, but found it difficult to find really suitable employment.

At their request I spent many hours counselling them about the difficulties they were facing as a family.

To enable the husband to find better employment I spent most Friday evenings helping him to translate difficult technical manuals from English to Japanese. I had placed myself at their disposal. I felt I was fulfilling my pastoral responsibilities towards them. We occasionally met for Bible study in their home and through this one of their neighbours had come to Christ.

There was, however, one thing that constantly bothered me. The wife never seemed happy in the worship service. She came a considerable distance on her bicycle, often in very bad weather. Her endeavour to be at the worship service was commendable, but she did not seem to enjoy being there. A cloud of heaviness seemed to hang over her.

From time to time I attempted to speak to her about this, but did not meet with a positive response. I had studied the differences between English and Japanese thought patterns. In my discussions with this couple I worked on the principle that it is best to avoid direct confrontation when counselling in Japan. Also, because this couple did not feel free to commit themselves to our fellowship by becoming members, I was especially careful in this respect.

Whenever I spoke to them about their Christian lives and their family circumstances I felt they were understanding the advice and counsel I was offering them, even though I spoke in an indirect manner lest I offended them.

For all my attempts to get at the heart of the problem, their general attitude did not change. This went on for some months and, even though the church was growing, this situation became a problem to me.

Imagine my joy then when, one Saturday afternoon, I received a phone call from the wife saying that she wished to talk with me heart to heart about her difficulties. Rejoicing that the opportunity we had prayed for had arrived, Sarah and I went to meet her and her husband at the church. While Sarah made some tea, the three of us sat together in the next room.

The wife was obviously very burdened and upset. She seemed reluctant to speak. In an effort to put her at ease I spoke first. I said just one simple sentence, but it resulted in a misunderstanding so great that the wife burst into tears and left the room.

All I said was, "I have waited a long time for this day to come".

What I meant was that I had prayed for the day when we could really talk openly together.

She, on the other hand, felt that I was judging her from a position of spiritual superiority They both left the church angry and upset.

Later they contacted me again, but only to state very clearly that in their opinion I had never loved or cared for them as a pastor should, that I had never rebuked them when they were obviously not honouring the Lord by their attitudes, and that I was full of nationalistic and spiritual pride. They concluded that I was not fit to be a minister of the gospel, let alone a missionary to Japan. The wife later stated that she had been testing me and had found me wanting.

I was devastated. It was a bitter, painful experience. It had never occurred to me that I would ever be accused like that by a Japanese Christian. My initial reaction was to think of all the time and effort I had expended on their behalf. In doing so I sought to assure myself that I had loved them in the Lord, but the bitterest experience was yet to come.

That night, unable to sleep, I sought comfort in the Scriptures. I looked for a word of encouragement from the Lord. I was hurt more deeply than I had ever experienced before. I felt sure the Lord would comfort me. I read passage after passage of Scripture deep into the night.

Early in the morning the Lord spoke clearly to me. I was reading John's Gospel 10:11-15: *I am the good shepherd: the good shepherd giveth his life for the sheep. But he that is an hireling and not the shepherd, whose own the sheep are not seeth the wolf coming and leaveth the sheep, and fleeth: and the wolf catcheth them, and scattereth the sheep. The hireling fleeth, because he is an hireling and careth not for the sheep. I am the good shepherd, I lay down my life for the sheep.*

Through these verses I was suddenly confronted with the fact that, concerning these two Christians, my motives were not pure at all. I really had failed them by not confronting them and challenging them as I should have. Under the guise of 'understanding the culture' I had not been prepared to risk my popularity in order to face them up to their dishonouring attitudes. I loved myself more than I cared for their spiritual wellbeing. I was not a true shepherd if I was not willing to die for the sheep.

This was the bitterest part, the Lord seemed to be agreeing with them! Rather than receive comfort I had received light. It was certainly not comfortable to be in such penetrating and revealing light!

I began to fear that others may have been similarly stumbled. What should I do? The Lord began to show me that, too! There, in the small hours of the morning the Lord challenged me to do something from which I shrank.

He challenged me to ask forgiveness of the fellowship. Later that morning the service would be followed by The Lord's Supper. This is where the Lord instructed me to make my confession to the church, to ask their forgiveness for not being a true shepherd to them, for not being willing to suffer for them.

This was very hard for me to contemplate. I had led most of them to Christ. They looked upon me as their spiritual leader. The Lord was calling me to confess to them. He was dealing with my pride. I determined to obey Him.

At the close of the worship service the members stayed behind to take part in The Lord's Supper. There were about ten in all. I read from John 10, testified of how the Lord had spoken to me, confessed my sin before them and asked their forgiveness. I also told them that with the Lord's help I would be a faithful shepherd to them, whatever they thought of me.

I found it a hard thing to do, but as I testified a remarkable thing took place. What followed remains indelibly imprinted upon my memory. Almost to a man, one after another the Christians began to weep. Even men wept quite openly. The Christians, too, began to pray prayers of confession. They told the Lord how they had not really prayed for Sarah and me as they knew they should. They in turn also began to pray for forgiveness.

The Holy Spirit did a thorough work in us all that day. We experienced a revival of joy and fellowship.

From that day on, Ritto church began to grow steadily, and for the next few years became one of the fastest-growing fellowships in our group of churches.

I have often reflected upon this bittersweet experience. The couple concerned never returned, although a measure of reconciliation was later achieved. I had learned a painful lesson, but the Lord, because He loves the church, had overruled and brought blessing to His people. He had brought beauty from ashes.

Looking back, I can now see that I grew more as a Christian and as a missionary during the hours of that experience than at any other time in my Christian life. And yet some fifteen years later I can hardly recall it without tears.

I had begun to learn an often-untaught church growth principle, that of brokenness in those who lead. If we humble ourselves, He will be exalted in our ministry. I had begun to really learn to die to my reputation. My reputation has meant little to me since that bitter yet blessed weekend.

It is better to die to self, obey Christ, and seek to be filled with the Holy Spirit. Only along this pathway will we be led to the rich experience of service with nothing to fear, nothing to hide, and nothing to prove. We are thus released to be ourselves, and yet also be wholly His.

The blessing at Ritto continued. A young man converted in a nearby town joined us. He witnessed to his older brother through tapes and books, but the older brother rejected the message and ridiculed his faith. He faithfully persisted in his witness. The older brother's health began to deteriorate. He began to think of the more serious issues of life.

One Sunday morning the older brother came, with his wife, to the fellowship at Ritto. They listened carefully. The message, based on the story of the widow who gave two coins, was about the nature of true faith and the need to believe Christ and trust Him for salvation. Though not my normal practice at the worship service, I felt I should make an appeal for response. Immediately the older brother raised his hand to indicate that he had received Christ. Almost simultaneously though a few seconds later, his wife did the same. They prayed there in their seats and then I prayed for them publicly. As they left the church I rejoiced with them at the fact that they had trusted Christ together. I also invited them to visit Sarah and me the following Tuesday for an evening meal together.

They arrived on the Tuesday evening with one burning question, "Pastor, which one of us indicated our desire to trust Christ first?"

I was a little bemused at the question. I asked them why they wanted to know. They explained that they had had their first argument as Christians on their way home from church. The wife had chided her husband with the words, "I don't want you to say you are a Christian just because I decided to be one!"

He replied, "But I indicated my desire to trust Christ before you did. I put my hand up first."

"Oh no you didn't," she responded "I put my hand up first." Thus they argued on their way home from their first visit to a Christian fellowship. Now they had come to visit, they were determined to find out who was first!

I told them the husband was first, but it was so close that they should consider themselves as having become Christians together. This seemed to please them both. The argument was over.

A little later the two brothers' mother put her faith in Christ and was baptised. The older brother later went to Bible school and became a pastor himself.

Mrs H., the hairdresser, continued a keen witness. She led one of her customers to the Lord. Also Mrs A's husband, who had vowed that he would never become a Christian, was converted. Joy's piano teacher, a young lady in her early twenties, also became a Christian. A small group of young teenagers began to attend the worship service. The Sunday school grew too, with up to thirty children attending each Sunday.

*The Ritto church building as it is today*

We now had a viable fellowship. At times thirty adults attended the worship service each Sunday morning. Men began to take on leadership responsibilities and one or two, after instruction, occasionally, preached.

Christians began to ask prayer for healing. Mrs A's son was healed of a kidney complaint after the believers met and prayed for him one

Sunday afternoon. A leadership group was formed and, just before we left for furlough, a young Japanese pastor was appointed to lead them. The church welcomed him as their pastor, and were able to support him financially from the beginning of his ministry. Under his leadership the Ritto church continued to grow. Land was purchased in a central location within sight of the local railway station, and a fine building was erected.

Ritto church continues its witness. The Lord built His church in Ritto. We look back on our six years there with much rejoicing.

Chapter Ten
# VILLAGE LIFE

Our own family also grew in Ritto. Joy began to play outside in the village. Her Japanese playmates were constantly in and out of the house. In fine weather she would come home covered in mud, having tried to catch crayfish in the local stream or, through her efforts, with her friends, to 'help' the farmers at work in the paddy fields.

If she were not in the streams or the fields, the next place to look for her would be in the shrine compound, where swings and a roundabout had been placed by the villagers for the local children.

The local shrine compound, which was next to the house in which we lived, was the social and religious focal point of the village. It was the children's playground. It was both safe and cool. Local traffic could not enter the compound. The tall pines and cedars which surrounded it provided good shade during the hot summers. Lines of stone lanterns provided clear markers for the many 'home runs' the boys scored during their games of baseball, the most popular outdoor sport in Japan. The girls were most likely to be found playing hide-and-seek around the dancing platform.

Local children grew up with a deep affinity with the local shrine. It was a symbol of safety, friendship, and village community as well as being the centre of village worship and administration.

Because of the spiritual darkness associated with such places, we considered forbidding our children to play there, but we decided against doing so. We taught the children to use it as a playground and nothing else.

Joy grew up speaking fluent Japanese, albeit the local, unrefined dialect with its many colloquialisms and less than elegant words! She always knew far more than Sarah and me, what was going on in the village! She was well liked by all the village families. Her popularity provided us with some embarrassing moments.

One day upon returning from a shopping trip in a nearby town, we drove up the narrow lane beside the shrine. In the compound there was a great deal of activity. The village harvest festival had begun. The shrine buildings had been decorated with streamers and bunting. Most of the villagers had gathered. Benches had been placed in rows before the shrine. The village elders and dignitaries, dressed in their best suits, sat in polite silence as the white-robed Shinto priest faced the crowd and waved his ceremonial purification wand of white paper streamers over them.

There, right in the centre of the front row, her pink clothes looking even brighter amidst the black and dark grey suits of the village elders, sat Joy, trying with all her might to imitate the poker-faced expression of sombre dignity displayed by the old men on her right and her left. All the other village children were with their parents at the back of the gathering where they belonged.

It looked so odd to see a brightly-dressed English five-year-old surrounded by all the village dignitaries, but they seemed glad to have her with them and were certainly looking after her. As for Joy she knew that after the ceremony there would be freshly boiled rice with sweet bean paste for all and sundry. She was determined to get her share!

We called her away as politely as we could. At home we explained why she should not have been there. She in turn assured us that she would have said, "Thank you, Jesus, for this food," before she ate the rice and bean paste!

The children often brought stray kittens home. They found and befriended them at the shrine next door. We would not allow them to keep the kittens at the house - we would have been overrun with cats in no time at all - but we encouraged the children to be kind to the kittens. Sarah often gave the children titbits to feed to them. There were many strays at the shrine compound. Local people abandoned unwanted pets there because they knew they would help themselves to any food offered before the stone idols and therefore not go completely hungry This helped to salve the conscience of those who threw the animals away.

One day Ruth, our second daughter; returned home from playing at the shrine compound and confronted Sarah with this question, "Mummy, do little kittens like fish?"

They certainly do," Sarah replied, "but why do you ask?"

"Oh, I thought they liked fishes, too," said Ruth, "I saw some fishes swimming in the river, so I put a kitten in the river so it could catch some."

Unknown to Ruth I went along the bank of the stream until I found. the drowned kitten. Then I buried it.

I have often used this incident in my sermons to explain to the Japanese that sincerity alone is not enough. Indeed, sincerity alone can be a dangerous thing. It could cost life, even eternal life.

After less than two years in Ritto it was time to begin Joy's formal education. We had already decided that the children would be educated in English. For this reason we did not send them to the local Japanese nursery school. Any English they had would have disappeared that much quicker. The children were naturally fluent in Japanese. We felt their English would suffer even further if we sent them to Japanese primary school. Also, we knew it would help them to settle into school on furlough if they were used to studying in English.

Using a home-teaching course from London, Sarah began to instruct Joy each morning while Ruth accompanied me on my pastoral and evangelistic visiting in Ritto town and the surrounding villages and housing estates. By this time she also had her childhood friends in the village of Ohashi.

The witness of a Christian family in a non-Christian culture is very rewarding and exciting. The children, with their natural gifts of friendship and their ability to put strangers at ease, are themselves vital and fruitful members of the missionary team.

All our children's friends began to attend Sunday school.Even when we moved the Sunday school from Ohashi to the new premises at the other side of Ritto, they still continued to attend.

We found our neighbours in Ohashi to be kind, courteous and friendly. In general we seemed to get on well with them, but living in a traditional Japanese village community brought us face to face with customs and beliefs which made life difficult at times.

The Japanese sense of obligation made it difficult to be spontaneously kind to our neighbours. All acts of kindness, especially by outsiders like ourselves, had to be repaid as a matter of duty.

The young couple who lived directly behind us both went to work each morning after their children had left for school. The wife worked half days and was usually home by afternoon. On bright sunny days she would often leave the bed quilts out in the garden, spread over long bamboo poles, to air. They made a colourful sight with their red and gold patterns gleaming in the sunlight. Occasionally the weather would take a turn for the worse before the young wife returned home. It would begin to rain. Sarah, because she did her own laundry at the back of the house, would be the first one to see the beautiful quilts getting wet. She would rush out the house and bring in the quilts before they got really wet.

After folding them neatly she took them to the young housewife as soon as she returned from her work. Within a matter of minutes the young wife or her mother, who also lived in the village, would arrive on our doorstep with profuse apologies and a gift, usually cream cakes or a box of soaps. This happened so often it became embarrassing. Yet it was not possible for Sarah to stand by and see the beautiful quilts getting wet.

A compromise solution was found. Sarah would fold the quilts and place them carefully in the porch of the neighbour's house where they would get neither wet nor dirty. The neighbour was under no illusion as to who had done this, but she could not be absolutely sure. She was therefore under no obligation to bring Sarah any gift. For Sarah to have continued to rescue the quilts, bring them into our house and later present them to the lady next door, would have resulted in us becoming real nuisances rather than good neighbours.

Sadly one morning while both the husband and the wife were at work and the children at school, the house next door burned to the ground. Sarah discovered the fire first, while it was still contained inside the house. She saw the flames through her lace curtained windows. She raced round the village shouting, "Fire! Fire!"

The fire took hold rapidly. Valuable minutes were lost because the village roads were too narrow for the modern fire engine to traverse. A hand drawn pump, kept at the shrine, was pressed into service. The village men worked quickly and efficiently. They fixed one end of the hose in the local stream and pumped water from the stream onto the fire, but the battle was lost before water reached the flames in any measure.

As the heat from the fire intensified the windows of our house began to crack, the plastic guttering to twist and melt. I trained the garden hose on our house to try to keep the temperature down. A breath of wind in our direction would have set our house ablaze, as the houses were only a few yards apart The house next door burned down completely. It was a sad day for the village.

Almost as great as their concern for their own daughter and son-in-law, who had lost their home and possessions, was the concern of the aged parents of the young couple for Sarah. There is a deep-seated superstition in the villages of rural Japan that if a pregnant woman is the first to discover a fire, she will either lose the baby or it will be born badly deformed. Sarah was eight months pregnant with our third daughter, Ann. The mother of the lady next door was distraught.

She was very worried about Sarah and the unborn child. She came to Sarah with the earnest promise that she would pray every morning and night to the gods and the buddhas that Sarah and the baby would be safe. We thanked her for her sincere concern, but also assured her that all was in the hands of our Heavenly Father. When Ann was safely born, well and healthy the old lady was greatly relieved.

The whole village was mobilised to clear up the charred remains of the house next door. Without any obvious instructions everybody seemed to know what to do. I helped shovel charred and sodden timber onto a waiting lorry. A bulldozer was borrowed from the local Caterpillar Company. By nightfall the site was levelled. Fresh sand was spread over the ground to hide any trace of the fire. Within a few hours of the fire a stranger would not have known that a house had stood on the site. After everyone had bathed in their homes, most of the men met at the shrine to drink *sake* and commiserate with the young couple and their parents. I, too, returned home and cleaned up, thankful that our house had been spared. We felt the ordeal was now over, but it was not so.

The following day, while speaking to the neighbour who lived in the house to the immediate east of ours and next to the house that had burned down, we found he was both angry and worried. He said he was very sorry that the young couple had lost their home, but was also very upset at the way the charred remains had been cleared up. He declared that they had not been cleared up properly. Every-one had omitted something extremely important. If it was not done soon it would surely result in further tragedy very quickly.

I thought he was being unreasonable. I told him everyone had worked hard to clear up the site. He then began to explain his concern.

What had upset him was that in their haste to clean up the site before nightfall no one had called the local Shinto priest to hold a purification ceremony over the spot where the toilet had been. According to our neighbour, who was a fifty-year-old salaried man working in the city of Osaka, the 'god of the toilet' could be very spiteful when not appeased or treated correctly. Because of this, he was quite certain that some calamity would befall either his house or ours if something was not done quickly. Our houses were the only two that faced directly on to the one that burned down. He was sure we were in considerable danger.

He said he would do something himself, but because the sand had been spread so quickly and thickly neither he, nor anyone else, could exactly identify where the toilet had been. I was astonished at his sincerity. He was truly fearful, and he a businessman in modern Japan!

I assured him he need not be concerned for our safety, for we trusted in One who was well able to protect us from such things. I urged him to do the same, but to no avail.

Very soon after these events his eldest son, a tall young man, physically healthy though slightly mentally unbalanced, died suddenly during the night!

Three or four times a year every village household sent one adult to the shrine compound to form a working party which cleaned up the whole village. Streams were dredged, weeds cut back, rubbish cleared from public places, fences mended and the shrine compound tidied. This activity always began on Sunday morning. The working party gathered at the village shrine at 8.00am. There they received their allotted tasks and orders for the day. This coincided with our busiest time of the week! Sunday school started at 9.00am. but we ferried children by car from the village well before then. There was no way that either Sarah or I could take part. When the working party was at its busiest, we were just starting the morning worship service.

I went to the village elders and offered to do my stint of dredging or cutting back weeds on a Saturday. My offer was not accepted. The elders explained that if one person in the village did their stint on Saturdays others would want to do the same. Village solidarity would suffer. There was nothing for it but to pay the fine levied upon any household which did not contribute an adult member. There always seemed to be one or two villagers knee deep in water outside our house as we set out for Sunday school. We felt a little embarrassed about this, but our priorities were obviously different. There was nothing we could do.

We sought to show our village solidarity in other ways. Some of the local mothers understood our feelings and confided privately, "Do not be too concerned. You do your part by taking the children to Sunday school. It keeps them out of our way for a couple of hours while we get on with the work!"

Our life in Ohashi was full and happy. The children had many friends in the village. They enjoyed their time there. Although as foreigners, we could never be an integral part of village life, we were not made to feel unwelcome. Our neighbours helped us in many useful ways. They knew that our stay m the village would not last many years, but our children endeared us to many of them. They did their very best to make us feel at home among them.

Because we were living in a completely Japanese environment we used the Japanese language constantly. I preached in Japanese three or four times a week. I did much of my preparation from Japanese books. We regularly introduced Japanese Christian literature to the fellowship and read most of it ourselves first.

I had sat and passed A level Japanese and one other subject. This gave me an idea concerning future language study. I knew I needed some external stimulus to help me keep up a systematic study of the language. The busier we became, the easier it was to relegate language study further down the scale of priorities. I knew that without some long-term objective, language study would be squeezed out of the weekly programme entirely.

I decided to enrol as an external student with London University and enter for a first degree in Japanese.

Armed with a book list and some old degree examination papers, for the next five years I worked steadily through all the aspects of the degree examinations. This long-term objective gave me the stimulus I needed. It forced me to study Japanese history and literature as well as language. To cover the syllabus I went back to language school in the city of Kyoto for four hours a month. With a private teacher I studied the composition of Japanese correspondence and the grammar of classical Japanese. I also encountered Japanese poetry for the first time.

Thus I continued to visit the language school and progress in my study of Japanese. I was still a language student for the whole of our second term!

Towards the end of our time in Ritto we became very busy missionaries indeed. The fellowship had grown and needed nurture and ministry. Our family had grown, too. We now had two daughters to teach every day and one to keep occupied. We had become leaders of the WEC missionary fellowship, and deputy leaders of the Japanese fellowship of churches. We had become busier than we could ever have imagined, but with good health and the joy of seeing a work of God grow in the place where He had placed us, we pressed on rejoicing. We look back on our six years in Ohashi village, Ritto, with much thanksgiving.

Since those days it has become an increasing source of amazement to me that so few Christian young people come forward to embark on this, one of the greatest of all adventures - cross-cultural evangelism which results in the formation of Christian fellowships in places where there is yet no church.

*A typical small, Japanese church building.*

## Chapter Eleven

# HOME AGAIN

After six years in rural Japan furlough was an exciting prospect, but twelve years as missionaries had brought considerable changes to our family needs. There were now five of us. Furloughs for missionary families need considerable thought and planning.

Having both been brought up in rented flats, neither Sarah nor I had a home of our own. Both our fathers had died. Our brothers and sisters had all married and left home. Our mothers lived in smaller council accommodation. The homes we were brought up in were no longer home to either of us. We were faced with the problem of where to live for the fifteen months of our furlough.

The little flat above the mission hall in Deptford was now too small for our needs. In any case, it was by this time occupied by the assistant pastor and his family. We wanted to be close to the mission hall in order to strengthen the bond of fellowship with our friends there. We needed a family house in south-east London at a reasonable rent. Not an easy proposition at all!

Another practical problem for a family with three young children was that of arranging school for them from halfway round the world. With no address in the UK, it was not possible to apply to a local school. Furthermore, we wanted all three of our daughters to go to the same primary school. They spoke to each other and played together using the Japanese language. They would need each other for the first three months at least.

It is in the face of problems like these that the practical help of the missionary's home church is invaluable. How grateful we were to the little group of Christians at the mission hall and friends we had made there in the past. Months before we were due to arrive in the UK, the mission hall secretary was writing letter after letter to other missionary societies and Christian groups asking if they had any rentable property in southeast London. As a result of these efforts a house was found in Eltham, southeast London. It was available for most of our planned furlough.

As soon as we had an address, friends visited the local Church of England primary school and made applications on behalf of our three children. Others arranged a reliable second-hand car for us, while yet others opened their own homes to us while we waited to move into our furlough house. The mission-hall fellowship also pledged to pay half the rent for the house.

The mission hall itself had been through troubled times while we were away in Japan. It had not been easy for the fellowship there, as they struggled for their very existence amidst a continually deteriorating inner-city situation. Although never able to support us financially to any great extent, their support had been faithful, consistent and sacrificial. They had never ceased to pray for us.

The way they showed their concern for us as we approached furlough was the true measure of their commitment towards us. It was worthy of any larger and more prosperous church. The warmth of their love and fellowship was a great encouragement to us.

Six years in Ritto, with its many and varied responsibilities, had left us quite tired. We were not ill, but we were physically weary. It was so helpful to have so many practical details looked after for us as we anticipated re-entry into UK society. Blessed is the missionary family whose home church and friends concern themselves with the many practical problems that furlough presents. We were blessed indeed.

The house which was found for us was a large four-bedroomed, semi-detached, family dwelling in a quiet road just a few minutes walk from the local shopping centre and the primary school. The four bedrooms were upstairs. The downstairs rooms included a large lounge, a study, dining room and kitchen. Sixty feet of garden extended behind the house. After the small rooms of our home in Ritto, the house in Eltham seemed enormous. Before moving in, we travelled to Scotland to visit Sarah's family and have a holiday with friends in Inverness.

While we were with our friends in Inverness all three children went down with whooping cough at the same time. Night after night we were awakened by the distinctive rasping induction of air which heralds a coughing and vomiting attack. Up we would leap from our beds, race to the adjoining room, buckets and towels in hand, hoping we would get to the right child first and in time. Our hosts were marvellous in their patience and understanding. The children were quite amazing too in their determination not to let the whooping cough spoil their holiday. They revelled in the novelty of sleeping in beds, eating what to them was strange food, and discovering British television. They also enjoyed being a novelty themselves, as they chatted away to each other in fluent, rural Japanese. Not even the whooping cough could diminish their enthusiasm. They were determined to miss nothing.

Holidays and visiting over, we travelled down to southeast London to begin a more settled existence in the house in Eltham. Joy, Ruth and Ann, who had all shared the same tiny room in Japan, were thrilled to have bedrooms of their own for the first time in their lives. They were also looking forward to going to a real school. We had timed our furlough so that Ann, our youngest, would start school with her sisters. It was important that during furlough she get a good educational base in English, upon which she could build through the home-teaching course we would use when we returned to Japan for the third time.

Before the commencement of the school year we paid a visit to the school to explain to the headmaster, and to the form teachers responsible for our daughters, some of the linguistic difficulties our children would face. The difficulties would arise from the fact that, although our children could understand and speak English, their thought patterns were most definitely Japanese. They used their English in the same way they used their Japanese.

Among other things this meant that they answered questions according to their grammatical construction, rather than with a 'Yes' or 'No' based upon their personal intentions or knowledge. This would bring all kinds of confusion when asked a negative question.

If asked, "Don't you know the answer?" they would reply 'Yes" if they did not know the answer (That is, "Yes I agree with you, I do not know the answer." They would answer "No" if they did know the answer, (i.e. "No, you are wrong I do know the answer") It is not difficult to imagine how utterly confusing this would be for both student and teacher alike. Without some explanation from us there would be no way the teachers could guess what was happening in our children's minds!

The children continued to play in the Japanese language. They used it among themselves most of the time. This often amused our friends and occasionally provided us with some embarrassing and humorous incidents.

One such incident involved an elderly lady on a train. Initially she was far from amused. We had been for a day out to London. The children had thoroughly enjoyed the pigeons in Trafalgar Square, had politely followed Sarah and me through the National Gallery and had been excited by some of the things they had seen in the shops in Regent Street. Now we were on our way home. The train from Charing Cross was crowded with rush-hour commuters, but we managed to squeeze into a carriage. Men looked over the tops of their evening papers, and those who had begun to doze off to sleep opened their eyes at the sound of three little English girls jabbering away in a language which was foreign to most ears in Britain. Joy Ruth and Ann were talking excitedly to each other, in fluent Japanese, about all they had seen. Sarah and I spoke to them in English whenever their volume became too loud, or when we wanted to explain something to them, but they replied in Japanese. Most people in the carriage were bemused by this, but once the novelty had worn off they went back to their newspapers or nodded off to sleep. They had given up trying to guess which language the children were using. That is, all except an elderly lady sitting in a corner seat by the window. She seemed upset, agitated by the children. As the journey continued her face became a mask of concern.

As the train moved out towards the suburbs more and more people got off at each station. Eventually only the elderly lady and the five of us remained in the carriage.

The children, with the carriage to themselves, were looking out of one window and then the next, still chatting away in Japanese. After one particular stop, the train made an exceptionally smooth start as it pulled away from the station. So smooth was the start that Ann, the youngest, did not realise the train was moving. Suddenly she cried out, "Miteyo miteyo ki ga ugoite iru ki ga ugoite iru!" ("look, look, the trees are moving, the trees are moving!") As she said this she pointed towards the window where the elderly lady sat. She was visibly upset.

Thinking that Ann had offended her by pointing in her direction Sarah spoke to her, explaining that Ann did not intend to be rude but was pointing at the trees and not at her. She also explained that the children had been brought up in Japan and were using the Japanese language. In an instant the elderly lady's face was a picture of relief. She began to smile and said, "Oh, I am so glad you told me. You see, recently my eyesight has begun to deteriorate. Listening to you and your children I thought my ears had begun to play tricks on me too!"

She left the train with a spring in her step!

The children settled down to school life very quickly. Only those who have experienced the discipline and patience that is needed to educate ones own children at home for years will understand the sheer delight it was to see them go off happily to school each morning. They also began to attend the Girls' Brigade and Explorers' Club at the local Baptist church which we all attended on Sunday mornings. This helped them to make friends quickly. It also helped towards a speedy integration into every-day life in Britain. This church, too, received us gladly and showed much love and understanding towards our children.

One enormous encouragement to us at this time was the mission hall in Deptford. Deptford had continued to deteriorate but during our six years in Ritto remarkable things had happened at the Shaftsbury Christian Centre.

Shortly after our return to Japan a pastor had been called to lead the work of the mission hall. Mr Victor Jordan, with his wife Jean, accepted the challenge of Deptford. With their four young children they moved into a house near the mission hall.

Pastor Jordan, reflecting on his early days in Deptford, described them in the following words:

*"We came to Deptford in 1975. We were joined by a deaconess and an assistant pastor and his wife. The purpose of this team ministry, as far as the committee was concerned, was to have one last attempt at evangelism by supporting this team, using the income that the mission received from various investments. When we arrived in Deptford a massive slum-clearance programme was in progress. This resulted in tremendous upheaval for the local people.*

*As a team we initiated a wide range of evangelistic activity - which was to no avail. Discouragement set in. The deaconess left after eighteen months. By early 1977 the assistant pastor was feeling a call to move elsewhere. As for myself I was ready to give the whole thing up! Discouragement in the work, disagreement in the committee which sought to lead the work, and division in the fellowship, increased as time went by. Years of working to a set pattern had resulted in resistance to any radical change. Discouragement had sapped faith. Without faith new direction was difficult.*

*In July of 1977 a conference was arranged in order to spend time together and try to work out a plan to remedy the situation. My brother Graham, a Baptist pastor, was asked to speak at this conference. We thought he would have ideas to share with us from his experience as head of department in a comprehensive school in the adjacent borough of Lewisham, a borough with problems similar to those in Deptford. Instead he spoke on the subject 'What God does when revival takes place.' In his final session he confronted us with this question, 'Could God bring revival to you in Deptford?'*

*This challenge resulted in the nine remaining members praying every week for God to do some thing in our lives that would give us new power. One by one we were all baptised in the Holy Spirit.*

*This quickly resulted in a transformation. At the summer camp for young people 17 out of 21 were converted. Such was the power of God at work in these newly-converted young people, and in us, that prayer continued, and numbers at the fellowship began to grow. The dryness which had been a feature of the meetings was dispelled almost overnight. It was replaced by enthusiasm and energy.*

*We expected God to be present. Worship became our joy. We began to see ourselves as a centre for evangelism, Bible teaching and worship, a community of Christians who were themselves a people of God with the necessary spiritual gifts to increase in numbers and holiness. We no longer saw ourselves as a mission hall dependent upon assistance from elsewhere, but as a church with its life and strength coming from within its fellowship".*

Six years earlier Sarah and I had returned to Japan concerned that we would perhaps have no home church to return to. Now, on the contrary, we saw that even in Deptford growth was possible.

Our testimony of what the Lord had done for us in Japan further encouraged the fellowship in Deptford. Together we were proving that He that is within us is greater than he who is in the world. (See 1 John 4:4.)

Once settled into our furlough house, the children at school, the Shaftesbury Christian Centre experiencing growth and knowing the joy of encouagement in the Lord, we began to rejoice at what was going to be, in many ways, an ideal furlough.

After a time of readjustment and rest we began a busy deputation programme. Each weekend I preached in different churches in and around London. In addition to this, I made trips of three weeks' duration to Scotland and the northeast of England. During the summer we took part in WEC youth camps, where we presented a programme depicting life and evangelism in Japan.

During a WEC children's camp in Dorset it was our privilege to give Bible talks to the children, and see our eldest daughter stay behind to be led to faith in Christ.

At another camp in North Wales gales lashed the campsite for days on end. Most men were up each night trying to keep the big marquee from blowing away! In the early hours of one morning, as we lay exhausted from the battle with the wind and rain, our own family tent suddenly split across the roof. The rain poured in upon us. The children, still half asleep, scrambled into other peoples tents. Sarah and I quickly dressed and tried to keep other tents from blowing away. It was a hectic, tiring camp, but the things we remember most are not the wind, rain and mud but the spiritual impact of the ministry at the camp. The fellowship displayed by staff and children in the battle to keep the camp programme going throughout our predicament was truly wonderful. The ministry was greatly aided by this. Many understood and responded to the good news of Christ and to the challenge of missionary service. It was hard work, but one of the highlights of our furlough.

During these often-busy months I continued my study of the Japanese language, seeking to prepare myself for the pending degree examinations. Two weeks before the exams took place Sarah kindly took the children to Scotland to give me some peace and quiet in which to revise. Even so, it was not with a great deal of confidence that I made my way to London University for the second time in my life.

I had received no tuition, I had attended no lectures. My efforts had neither been seen nor evaluated by anyone. With past examination papers as my only guide to the scope of study required, I was unsure whether I had covered enough ground or spread my studies too widely The memory load was high, 2,000 Chinese characters, many with a variety of phonetic readings, had to be retained if I was to do reasonably well.

It had been a useful discipline to keep me at my language-study books; I had also learned a great deal about Japanese history and literature, but as the day to return to the university to begin the examinations approached, my old feelings of inferiority concerning that place made themselves felt.

However, having committed myself to take the examinations, and having paid the examination fee, there was nothing for it but to go and do my best. I was glad when the ten days of exams were over. I then began to look forward to Sarah's and the children's return from Scotland.

After six months in the UK the children were speaking English to one another and doing well at school. They looked so typically English in their grey skirts, white blouses and maroon and gold neckties. When we saw them off to school each morning it was difficult to imagine that they had spent most of their lives in a completely different culture in the other side of the world, yet Sarah and I were already planning for our return to Japan.

We arranged for home-study courses to be sent to Japan for all three girls. We sent off numerous parcels of reading material and textbooks to our headquarters in Shiga prefecture. We even purchased a complete set of The Children's Encyclopedia Britannica and dispatched it, too, to Japan to await our arrival. The year at school in England was very good for the children. Their English improved tremendously, and their school work was well up to standard.

Blessed with good health and with the Lord supplying all we needed for our return, and with a rousing send-off from our friends at the Shaftesbury Christian Centre in Deptford, we set off for our third term of service.

Flying the shorter route over the pole, we arrived back in Shiga prefecture in September 1979.

## Chapter Twelve
# ISHIYAMA, THE STONE MOUNTAIN

The team of missionaries and pastors in Japan had made preparations for our third term of ministry. They had chosen Ishiyama (Stone Mountain) as our place of service. Accommodation had been rented for us, so we moved into Ishiyama very soon after arriving back.
For a family of five this was a tremendous help. We were grateful to belong to a fellowship which dealt with so many of the practical and logistical matters which accompany life as a missionary family.
The fellowship of missionaries and pastors in Japan was somewhat unique within WEC International. The churches which grew out of the early evangelistic endeavours of WEC missionaries had formed themselves into an association of local churches, with their own leadership and administration. Missionaries were invited back to Japan by this fellowship and integrated into it. We became members of the Japanese church.
The team of missionaries was truly international. During our third term the team consisted of missionaries from America, Brazil, Canada, Australia, New Zealand, Germany, Holland and Zimbabwe. All were integrated into the Japanese fellowship. Such a multi-cultural team itself is a living testimony to the power of the gospel. It was a privilege to be sent out by this Japanese-led fellowship into church planting in Ishiyama.
Ishiyama, though quite different from Ritto, was typical of much of modern Japan. It was a mixture of the old and the new. Though at one

time a separate community, it had been engulfed by the city of Otsu, and had become its most southerly suburb.

Otsu, the capital of Shiga prefecture, is a city of over 200,000 people. Hemmed in on the east by Lake Biwa, Japan's largest lake, and on the west by a range of hills, Otsu had extended along the banks of the lake to become one of the longest and narrowest cities in Japan.

Ishiyama lies at the extreme south of the city where the lake narrows and becomes the Seta River, which flows into the great metropolis of Osaka some sixty miles to the south. Ishiyama is the site of the oldest bridge over the Seta River. This made it a very strategic place in the history of Japan, because the Seta River had to be crossed from the east at Ishiyama in order to reach the old imperial capital of Kyoto, a further 15 miles to the west.

Central to the history of Ishiyama is its ancient Buddhist temple. Ishiyama temple has a recorded history of well over 1,000 years. Part of the famous novel, *The Tale of Genji* (the first novel in the history of world literature), is said to have been written in a room in Ishiyama temple towards the end of the tenth century AD.

People from all over Japan, indeed from all over the world, come to visit this old and famous temple with its beautiful gardens, ancient buildings, and moon-viewing platform, from which many prominent personages in Japanese Imperial Court history have stood gazing at the moon while composing classical court poetry in its praise.

We lived just a short walk away from this ancient and very influential temple, in a modern block of flats, on the fourth floor. From our front door we looked out on two other much smaller temples and a Shinto shrine, all within a hundred yards of our new home.

Being on the growing edge of the city, a completely contrasting view presented itself from the windows at the rear of the apartment. Not one old building was to be seen. The rice fields had been filled in and hills had been levelled. New houses, schools and shops extended to the south. Two worlds met in Ishiyama. The old traditional way of life centred on the soil, the temple and the shrine, and the newcomers who had purchased modern middle-class housing in which to bring up their families, while husbands and fathers commuted to Kyoto and Osaka.

Ishiyama was an enjoyable place in which to live. The river and hills provided pleasant surroundings. There was no local industry of any kind. Good commuting facilities, and proximity to Osaka, increased the popularity of Ishiyama as a dormitory town.

We were to discover, however, that the business and economic aspirations of the newcomers made them almost as difficult to reach with the gospel as the more traditional and conservative families. The influence of Buddhism and Shintoism on both groups was very strong. None would become Christians easily. From the spiritual point of view Ishiyama was aptly named. To us it was to become a mountain of stone indeed.

We settled in with enthusiasm. Our first task was to get our three daughters into their study programmes. Four desks were purchased. They literally filled one of our tiny rooms. This room became the school. Every morning from Tuesday until Saturday lessons began at 8.30am. Joy(1O), Ruth (8) and Ann (6) sat at their desks dressed in their Eltham Church of England school uniforms. I taught Maths, English, Science and Japanese until 10.00 After a thirty-minute break Sarah taught all the other subjects until 1.00pm. Three afternoons a week all three girls went to Japanese teachers for art, calligraphy and piano lessons.

Because our flat was both home and school, it was important for the girls that they played outside as often as possible. If they did not, they would become completely tied to the home. They needed social contact with other children as part of their natural development. However Ann, in particular, had lost her Japanese language ability. She did not have sufficient to enable her to play outside with any measure of confidence.

The following conversation took place quite frequently during our first few weeks in Ishiyama "Ann, while the sun is shining why not play outside?

"But mother, I have no friends to play with"

"If you play outside you will soon make some friends."

"But mother, how can I make friends when I cannot understand the other children, or even speak to them?"

"If you play outside with the Japanese children you will soon remember all your Japanese again.

"But mother, I have no friends to play with."

Most missionaries go through the trauma of seeing their children struggle with constant cultural adjustments, but most children will quickly adapt if they are sure that home is a safe and loving place to return to.

There were many other young families living in the block of flats and in the nearby houses. Each of our daughters soon had their own little group of playmates. We became hosts to a constant stream of Japanese children, mainly girls, all intensely keen to see how their foreign friends lived in Japan. Most of them were surprised to find that our life style was very little different to their own. Our children all made some very good friends.

From time to time they stayed for a night or a weekend at their friends' homes. Later we returned the compliment. Through this we got to know a good number of families in the neighbourhood.

It soon became apparent that our children would do better with a schoolroom in a location other than our flat. Also, Sarah and I needed a room of our own rather than sleep each night on the living-room floor.

We searched in the immediate locality and found a small bungalow that was not being used. It was quite old, but only a few minutes' walk away from the flat. It had obviously not been lived in for some time. We contacted the owner, a local man, who said it was not for rent. He planned to pull it down and build a new house on the site. He was not sure when he would do this, but feared that if he allowed people to live in it, he might not be able to get them to move out when he wanted to start building. Upon hearing that we did not intend to live in the house, and only intended to use one room, he gladly let us use it for a nominal sum each month, on the condition that we vacated it as soon as he was ready to pull it down.

We accepted his conditions and promptly moved the desks, wall charts and other equipment into the largest and brightest room. From then on the children actually left the flat and 'went to school' each morning While all their friends made their way to the local primary school, Joy, Ruth and Ann, still in their Church of England school uniforms, made their way along a narrow path through the rice fields to the little house they knew as school.

The move proved to be a great improvement. Not only did it give us more living space in the flat, it helped the children to more clearly define our dual roles of parents and teachers. It also freed the school programme from any distractions (there was no telephone in the schoolhouse), and gave the children a greater sense of relief when school was over and they could go home, rather than simply moving into a different room. Renting the little house also meant that Sarah had the flat to herself while I was teaching and vice versa. We each needed this time alone for prayer and study.

The little house had some space around it in which the children could skip and play games outside during their break periods. For the small amount it cost us each month it was a great boon to us all.

Sarah and I were not the first WEC missionaries in Ishiyama. Years previously Miss Laura Robinson, our co-worker in Otsu, had taught at the Teachers' Training College there, and had rented an apartment in Ishiyama in order to be close to the students she taught. Another WEC missionary, Miss Elaine Henderson (later to become Mrs Kitamura), had also taught at the same college. With the help of Miss Janice Urquhart (later Mrs Edwards of WEC Taiwan), she had begun a Bible study among some ladies in the area. In an effort to further develop this work a small house had been rented and worship services begun. It was at this stage that Sarah and I began our ministry in Ishiyama.

We did not find it easy. One young lady had been converted through the witness of Miss Urquhart in Kyoto. It took her ninety minutes to reach Ishiyama from her home in the countryside. Most Sunday mornings she was able to attend the worship service. However, during our first year at Ishiyama very few people attended. There were occasions when Sarah and I, and our three children, were the only ones present. Sarah supplied the music, I led and preached, and our three daughters joined in the singing! Most Sunday mornings we were joined by two or three ladies, but if ten people (including the five of us) were present we would consider that a big meeting. The beginning of our ministry in Ishiyama reminded us of our early days in Ritto all over again.

Our children brought their friends to Sunday school. This was an encouragement to us, but on the whole our first year in Ishiyama was hard, discouraging and fruitless. No one was converted. There were no baptisms.

Japan can be a very frustrating place for the missionary. Religious freedom is guaranteed by the constitution and is a political reality. There are hardly any restrictions on preaching the gospel or teaching the Bible. Any socially-undisruptive method of evangelism is permissible. The problem for us was that, no matter what method was used, nothing seemed to happen!

People were kind, polite and friendly yet nonetheless resistant to the news we brought them. None would ever stop and listen to open-air preaching. People were either too busy or simply not interested. Door-to-door visitation evangelism was often frustrated by the electronic speaking systems installed in the gateposts of modern houses.

We did door-to-door work distributed thousands of tracts and invitations, and sought to do personal evangelism. It was all to no avail. The notice board outside the little rented house said, 'Christian Church. Worship Service 10.30am. All Welcome.' but hardly anyone came!

We were faced once more with the question, 'What do we do when all we think we can do has been done and yet there are no results at all?"

We were very busy. We had the children to teach. There were sermons to prepare, language study to be fitted in, missionary and fellowship meetings to attend, etcetera. Our time and energy were consumed by a variety of activities, and yet our primary purpose, to see the kingdom of God extended, was not being achieved. Most of our activities were either directly or indirectly geared to this end, yet this was the one thing that simply was not happening.

Our previous experience in Ritto had taught us not to despair, but after a year of no conversions and so little progress, discouragement, the old enemy of the church planter in resistant places, began to creep into our hearts.

There is only one answer to discouragement, it has to be refused in the name of Jesus. This we did. We sought to encourage ourselves in the Lord.

The words of Scripture which were of particular encouragement to me at this time were the words of Jesus to Peter in Matthew 16:18: *"I will build my church, and the gates of Hades will not overcome it. I will give you the keys of the kingdom of heaven; whatever you bind on earth will he bound in heaven, and whatever you loose on earth will he loosed in heaven"*.

These words of Jesus have become very precious to us in our ministry in Japan. The words 'I will build my church' are, first and foremost, a proclamation of authority. Here Jesus proclaims His authority in no uncertain terms. He proclaims His intent to build His church. He declares that even the authority of Satan cannot overcome His church. All church planting takes place in the context of an authority encounter. There is a clash between the authority of Christ and the authority of Satan. In some parts of the world this battle is fiercer than in others but, in every part of the world, church-planting ministry should be based upon the proclamation of the authority of Christ, no matter how hard the battle may be.

The authority of Christ to build His church is not merely an ultimate authority which will win out in the end, and therefore give us hope in the distant future. It is a present authority which gives us a basis for hope-filled ministry here and now.

Our years in Japan have taught us that, no matter how hard the battle might be, no matter how unyielding the surrounding authority of Satan might appear, no matter what form the authority of Satan might take (whether it be false religion, occult practices, atheistic materialism, cynical indifference or political opposition), it can be met and overcome by a ministry based upon, and flowing from the authority of Jesus Christ. He will build His church. The authority of Satan cannot thwart or overcome the intent of Christ. Because of Christ's proclamation of authority in relation to the building of His church, we can be confident of the inevitability of the church.

If Satan cannot overcome His authority then nothing can. This is the firm basis upon which the church planter ministers. Any other basis will prove to be unable to sustain the church planter in resistant places.

The words of Jesus, 'I will build my church' also contain a prophetic element. When Jesus spoke these words there was no church. Indeed, Matthew 16:18 contains the first direct Scriptural reference to the church.

These words are a prophecy of victory, spoken into a situation which the disciples were to interpret as one of defeat and despair. In verse 21 of Matthew 16 we have the words, *"From that time on Jesus began to explain to his disciples how that he must go to Jerusalem and suffer... and be killed."*

The 'time' here refers to verse 16, the confession of Peter, *"You are the Christ, the Son of the living God"*. It was when this foundational truth of the church, the knowledge that Jesus Christ is indeed Lord of heaven and earth, was given to Peter by the Father that Jesus began to teach his disciples about the impending suffering, death and resurrection which awaited Him in the near future.

Christ's words concerning His immediate future in Jerusalem were fulfilled. He suffered and died. Faced with the fact of the death of Jesus, and the seemingly awful finality of the sealed tomb, the disciples were filled with fear and despair. They hid themselves away in a locked room because they were afraid. It was into this humanly-speaking hopeless situation that Jesus had prophesied His victory over Satan, *"I will build my church; the gates of Hades will not overcome it."*

The words 'gates of Hades' are translated as 'not even death' in the Good News Bible. Death, the ultimate power of Satan, could not overcome Jesus Christ. Neither could it prevent the birth of His church. When Jesus died upon the cross, He *tasted death for every man* (Heb. 2:9). *God made him who had no sin to be sin for us, so that in him we might become the righteousness of God* (2 Con 5:21). When Jesus died upon the cross He was exposed to the ultimate authority and power of Satan, yet He was victorious. He proved His power and authority historically, here on earth.

The words 'I will build my church ... the gates of Hades will not overcome it' remain prophetic for today. Jesus has not ceased to build His church. The fulfillment of this prophetic word began on the day of Pentecost when the church was born, but has yet to be completely fulfilled.

All around us may be discouraging. Humanly speaking the situation may appear impossible, but we must live and minister from within this prophetic word, in the assurance of its continuing historical fulfillment today.

In this way these words of Christ are a great encouragement to the church planter in resistant places. I have come to believe that insofar as the Lord has commissioned me to any particular place in Japan to see His church come into being then it is my privilege to live within the sure fulfillment of this prophetic word, just as it is my strength to minister from within its authority.

The words of Christ, 'I will build my church' are also a promise to be claimed. Jesus spoke these words specifically to Peter. The glorious confession of Peter, *"You are the Christ the Son of the living God,"* is the foundational truth upon which the church of Christ is built. It is not the person of Peter which is the rock but rather the profession of Peter concerning Christ.

There is, however, a sense in which Peter and his ministry was foundational to the early church. It was Peter who first preached the gospel of Christ to both Jew (Acts 2) and Gentile (Acts 10), and witnessed conversions among both groups. It was through Peter's ministry that the church was founded among both Jew and Gentile. Yet like so many of the promises of Scripture this promise has both a timely and a timeless application. It was a specific promise to Peter for a particular time in history, and yet it remains a promise which we can claim today.

We have, then, the words of Jesus, *'I will build my church'*; as a proclamation of His authority; a prophecy of His victory and a promise to His servants.

They are a source of great strength and encouragement when our circumstances seem to be hopeless.

The five words 'I will build my church' are not difficult to understand grammatically, yet I must confess that in my early days in Japan I did not really understand them. When Jesus says 'I will build my church' He means exactly that! Conversely it can be stated that in a very real sense no missionary, pastor, teacher or evangelist ever builds the church of Jesus Christ. This privilege belongs only to Christ Himself. It is He who builds.

This was a revelation to me, for in my early days as a missionary I was under the false impression that I was going to do it. In my enthusiasm I thought that building the church was my task. It was only after our experience in Ritto that I began to learn the painful lesson that I could not do it. There was no way in which my strength, my energy or my activity could ever be sufficient to see Japanese come to Christ and form a fellowship.

I am no match for Satan, but Jesus is! Praise His name, it is He who builds, not I.

What a tremendously liberating truth this is! It delivered me from the dreadful burden of seeking to appear successful as a missionary. My success or reputation has come to mean little to me. As long as Jesus builds His church, what do these things matter? They matter nothing at all!

Even though Paul describes himself as *'a wise master builder'*, we must always keep in mind that it is the Lord who *'adds to His church'* (Acts 2:47). We may arrange the 'bricks' but we certainly do not provide them!

The complete promise to Peter in Matthew 16:18-19 contains something of a paradox. It is Jesus who builds His church, and yet it is to Peter that He gives 'the keys of the kingdom of heaven'. Jesus will build His church, but it is the privilege and responsibility of the disciple to exercise the ministry of the keys, (i.e. the preaching of the glorious good news, the gospel of Christ) based upon the revelation given to Peter, 'Jesus is the Christ, the Son of the living God.'

Therefore, although Jesus will build His church, we cannot sit back and do nothing for we have been entrusted with the *'keys of the kingdom of heaven'*.

The keys of the kingdom of heaven, by which men and women have heaven's door thrown open to them, is the ministry of the gospel - the great privilege of declaring on the authority of Christ Himself, that men and women can be loosed from the penalty and power of sin and every other evil influence upon their lives. It also includes the tremendous responsibility of faithfully declaring that to refuse the offer of mercy proclaimed by the gospel results in the hearer remaining bound in sin, a captive of Satan.

The very fact that the ministry of the gospel is described as 'the keys of the kingdom of heaven' tells us something important about the gospel itself. If I give you the key to my house, I am giving you the authority to enter my house.

A key is a symbol of authority. Therefore the gospel should be ministered with authority. Whether it be in our personal witness, or from the pulpit, our testimony to what Christ has done, and to Who He is, should be 'with power'. While there is a legitimate place for Christian apologetics, there is no place, and no need, to apologise for the cross, the resurrection or the kingship of Christ. We must avoid bigotry, but also be filled with a godly confidence in the Lord and the gospel.

A key is also a symbol of freedom. If I give you the key to my house, I am not only giving you the authority to enter it, but also the freedom to enter whenever you like. You may open the door as many times as you wish.

We have been given the 'keys of the kingdom of heaven'. We should use them freely. Freely we have received, freely we should give. The gospel should be like a well of living water springing from our hearts and lives. We should be freely enjoying the grace of forgiveness, while ministering forgiveness to others. We should be rejoicing in the freedom of deliverance while ministering deliverance to others.

There should be a freedom about our witness and our ministry. Sharing Christ should be a natural part of our lives. The gospel should flow freely from us.

A key is also a symbol of suitability. A key is of no use unless it fits. The gospel is a wonderful key. It is a key that fits. In an international mission like WEC we see continually how the gospel of Jesus Christ, when preached in freedom, love and power, meets the heart needs of men and women, boys and girls, in all cultures, however diverse they may be.

No matter what the linguistic group, economic condition, educational standard, colour, race or customs, the gospel is a 'key which fits' the heart needs of all. What a privilege to be entrusted with such a key!

How great should be our confidence in this gospel and how great our determination to preach no other!

Here then is a Biblical basis for confidence in the church-planting missionary. He has a Master unto whom is given 'all authority in heaven and earth', a Master who will build His church in spite of all opposition.

*Patrick lectures at a PTA meeting*

The missionary serves from a position of imparted authority. He preaches a message of forgiveness and deliverance, which is indeed 'the power of God unto salvation to everyone who believes'. When the gospel is proclaimed from this position of authority, the church comes into being - as we shall see in Acts chapter two and in Ishiyama, where even 'stone mountains' would begin to yield.

Chapter Thirteen

# THE OUTWORKING OF
# THE PROMISE

---

The promise, *"I will build my church, and the gates of Hades will not overcome it. I will give you the keys of the kingdom of heaven"* ... began to be fulfilled on the Day of Pentecost, when the gospel was first preached by the disciples and the New Testament church brought into being.

In many respects what the Lord did on that day reveals to us the principles through which He continues to fulfill His promise and build His church throughout the world today.

In Acts 2:4-14 can be identified five basic principles which result in effective witness and evangelism which, in turn, results in the formation of new congregations. They can be listed as follows:

1.     The disciples were filled with the Holy Spirit.
2.     The disciples exercised spiritual gifts in their ministry and
        witness.
3.     Their witness was culturally relevant.
4.     They witnessed as a team.
5.     Their ministry was suited to their personalities.

The first principle is clear and obvious. For effective witness we must be filled with the Holy Spirit. There never has been, and there never will be, any substitute for this. No plans however well prepared, no strategy however wise, no effort however strenuous, no person no matter how abundantly gifted, can ever be a viable alternative to being filled with the Holy Spirit.

The second principle says that the public witness of the disciples on the Day of Pentecost was accompanied by and accomplished through the exercise of spiritual gifts. It is the exercise of spiritual gifts in evangelism and witness which makes us fruitful Christians.

On the Day of Pentecost the gift of the ability to speak in languages they had never learned was, in this instance, not primarily given to them for their mutual edification, but for their public witness. Through the exercise of this gift they told of 'the wonders of God' (VII). It was a miracle. It is also a principle. Effective evangelism is more dependent upon the ministry of spiritual gifts than it is upon well-thought-out plans.

The mistake we often make is to reverse the order. We draw up plans of evangelism, decide the activities, and then seek to encourage people to take part. We start with the plans and then think of the people. On the Day of Pentecost the order was different. Spiritual gifts were given, and then the 'open-air' began. We need to discern the spiritual gifts present in any group of Christians and then plan our strategies accordingly.

The third principle is that of cultural relevance. In verse 6 of Acts 2 we find that the combination of the infilling of the Holy Spirit, and the exercise of spiritual gifts in public witness, resulted in the disciples becoming culturally relevant to the different nationalities and linguistic groups present when the public witness began. Each person present 'heard them speaking in his own language' the wonderful works of God. They could understand the message.

The missionary serving in a culture other than his own is constantly searching for relevance in both linguistic competence and evangelistic method. The Holy Spirit understands all cultures. Because of this, when the method of proclamation is based upon spiritual gifts and other God given abilities, cultural relevance is made possible.

The fourth principle is that of teamwork. Although it was Peter who actually did the preaching (from verse 14 onwards), he did not stand alone. The other disciples stood with him. The very fact of their presence was a source of strength and encouragement. In most instances it is no more God's will that we should serve alone than it is that we should fellowship alone.

In pioneer work the trailblazer may have to serve alone in the beginning of a work but this should only be a temporary situation and not the norm. A team ministry should be developed as soon as possible, by either developing a ministry team from among converts, or by developing a team from among available missionaries and national full-time workers, or both. The whole of the book of Acts is a testimony to this principle.

The fifth principle is not obvious and may easily be overlooked. In verse 14 we read, 'Peter raised his voice' and proclaimed the gospel. Here he is speaking in his native tongue. This was no less the exercise of a spiritual gift.

When he finished, over 3,000 believed. The church was born. The promise in Matthew 16:1819 was fulfilled in its specific application to Peter. Peter had exercised the ministry of the 'keys'. Heaven's door was opened for others to enter. His ministry was based on the four principles listed above.

He is filled with the Holy Spirit

He is exercising a spiritual gift, that of preaching.

He is culturally relevant His message is for the Jews, and is filled with Old Testament references to which they could relate.

He stands as one of a team.

But why was it Peter who 'raised his voice'? Why not James, Andrew or John? The other disciples were there. They too, were filled with the Holy Spirit.

The first answer to this question is obvious. The promise in Matthew 16:18-19 was given specifically to Peter. Here he is fulfilling that promise. Also, there can be no doubt that Peter was one of the leaders, if not the leader, of the band of disciples. He may well have been the first to speak for this reason, too.

But alongside these reasons there is one more. It has to do with Peter's personality. Peter was constantly 'raising his voice' before anyone else! Time after time in the gospels we find Peter is speaking out before anyone else gets the chance! (e.g. Matt, 17:4, Matt, 19:27,

Matt, 26:33.)

Even in Matthew 16 Peter speaks first; in verse 16 where his answer is inspired and correct, and in verse 22 where his impulsive words draw the response from Jesus, 'Out of my sight, Satan'. Whatever the occasion, Peter was quick to react verbally. It was part of his personality to do so. On the day of Pentecost by 'raising his voice' he is being true to his personality. It was the personality that God had given to him, and even though he was filled with the Holy Spirit, he still had the same personality.

This is the fifth principle: be true to the personality God has given to you. He has not called you to copy someone else, or try to serve Him as if you were someone else. We should learn from others, but we should not try to copy them. We are each unique. Sadly the churches have in them many lovely quiet Christians trying their hardest to be extrovert and noisy while, on the other hand, many exuberant, outgoing people are trying to unnecessarily subdue themselves.

We do not need new personalities, we need Spirit-filled personalities. We can then be free to serve God as He intends us to. Because we are all unique, and because the Lord is also the Lord of our personalities, we can all be ourselves in our service for Him. We do not need to copy others, or try to live up to some ideal image of ourselves which we have created in our own mind. When we are truly liberated to be ourselves, and seeking to continually be filled with the Holy Spirit, others will see the reality of the work of God in us.

We should constantly seek to bring these five principles together in our ministry. It may not always be possible all the time to do this, but we should always be aiming at it.

When these five principles come together the Lord builds His church through us. Often He does this through ways we neither plan nor expect. This was our experience in Ishiyama where the Lord opened many different doors of evangelistic opportunity. In Ishiyama we saw more clearly how these principles worked out in our own lives and ministry.

"The Lord is utterly faithful but He is not predictable!" I do not know where I learned this phrase - I may even have constructed it myself - but it has certainly been a blessing and help to me. So often I have confused the Lord's faithfulness with the idea of predictability. I have learned, however, that in evangelism the Lord is full of surprises!

During our first year in Ishiyama no one was converted. Very few people attended the services, and even less with any kind of regularity. We were very busy. We sought to share Christ with those around us, but to no avail. We had learned not to give in to discouragement. We sought to make a fresh stand of faith. I sought to encourage myself through the promise of Jesus, "I will build my church, and the gates of Hades will not overcome it".

We reasserted our faith in His authority. We sought to place our hope in His prophetic word, and we claimed His promise to build His church in Ishiyama.

It is my experience that, whenever I make a fresh stand of faith for the future, things invariably get worse rather than better. It seems to me that this is some kind of spiritual law! After a fruitless year in Ishiyama we were trusting for some kind of breakthrough, but things got worse instead of better. We experienced a 'breakthrough' of the wrong kind!

About 11 o'clock one Friday night a man entered the church building. You may think that this should have encouraged us, but it did not. He went through the front doors of the little rented building without getting out of his car first! He was drunk and driving at speed. He entered the church at about sixty miles per hour. Not being a very substantial building in the first place, he made a real mess of it. It was completely unusable. Not only did he wreck the building but, sadder still, he killed a pedestrian on the steps in front of the building. As well as being a personal tragedy this also made the building taboo to the local Japanese. No one would be likely to enter the building for a year at least, especially if it remained a place of worship.

So, after one year of effort in Ishiyama, not only were there so few people coming, now they had no place to come to!

For a few weeks we met quietly in our apartment. It was far from suitable. Meetings of any kind were forbidden in the contract. Singing was out of the question. To meet there was obviously no solution.

The parents of one of our children's friends owned a little baker's shop which they had just stopped using. They offered it to us as a temporary meeting place. It was very small. About fifteen people could be seated if they squeezed up close to one another. It was more than ample for our needs. We were glad to be able to use it, but it was a discouraging time. The signs for bread and cigarettes were still up outside the shop. Occasionally a customer came in to try to make a purchase in the middle of the worship service. They certainly got a surprise! It was during this time of discouragement and transition that the Lord began to work on our behalf.

The unfolding of His plan began in an unusual place, the local barber's shop. I have always made it a practice to get my hair cut at the local barber's wherever I have lived in Japan. Barber's shops abound in Japan but they are very expensive compared to Britain. Although the service is good and thorough, a visit to the barber in Japan is six or seven times the price of a haircut in Britain! It is expensive, but it is also a good place to meet local men.

As soon as I entered the barber's shop I knew I was in the presence of a sportsman. The wallpaper was black and yellow stripes, the colours of the local professional baseball team. All over the wallpaper, written in black felt tipped pen, were the signatures of the players who made up the team known as the Hanshin Tigers.

Sure enough, when it was my turn the barber, a cheerful friendly man of about forty years of age began to speak about baseball. He spoke enthusiastically for about ten minutes, then stopped and asked me, "Aren't you interested in baseball?"

He had detected that my enthusiasm for baseball was not as great as his. I replied defensively, "Well, I have never played baseball, so I find it difficult to be very interested in the game."

"What!" he responded "You've never played baseball! Aren't you from America?" Like most Japanese he had assumed that, because my face is white and I speak English, I was an American.

"No," I replied, I am from England. We don't play baseball in England."

'Well," he said, "if you don't play baseball what do you play in England?"

'We play cricket in the summer, and football and rugby in the winter," I replied.

Thinking it might be similar to baseball, he began to ask me about cricket. I began to explain the system of runs and wickets, but he found it difficult to grasp. Trying to explain cricket to a Japanese must be one of the greatest cultural hurdles imaginable, rather like trying to explain the ethos of the Japanese tea ceremony to a Cockney! When asked how many hours an international cricket match lasted I told him, "Five days." That was the last straw. It was beyond his comprehension.

In those days most Japanese found it difficult even to take three consecutive days' holiday a year. He could not comprehend how a game with a bat and a ball could last five days, and even then probably end in a draw! We changed the subject and began to speak about football.

He detected an obvious love for football on my part by the way I spoke about it. He concluded that football was to me what baseball was to him. He then began to ask questions, 'Did you ever play football yourself?"

"Oh, yes," I replied. "As a boy, as a young man, and even when in the Air Force I played once or twice a week"

"Could you still pass the ball and head it? Could you referee a game?"
Yes, I am sure I could," I replied.

'You are the man we are looking for!" was his excited response.

He then went on to explain that he was the vice president of the local primary school sports club. He told me that they had fathers queuing up to teach and coach baseball, but there was no one to coach the boys in football. He then proposed that I become a football coach for the boys who wanted to learn.

"What would it involve?" I asked.

'Well," he said, "It's up to you, but what we would really like is for someone to give Saturday afternoons from one o'clock till five o'clock regularly throughout the year."

'Well, I am afraid I am not your man. I am too busy to give that much time," I replied

Saturday afternoon was when I often did my final sermon preparation for Sunday. There was hardly anyone coming to listen to the sermons, but I still had to have one ready!

The barber finished my hair and I went home. All through the week, whenever I prayed, the thought of becoming the boys' football coach came to my mind. So persistent was the thought that I went back to the barber and told him I would do it for one year. I ended up doing it for the remaining four years we lived in Ishiyama.

I was appointed coach to the younger boys, but was often in charge of them all. Every Saturday afternoon I had a group of boys numbering between thirty and fifty. We did passing and shooting practice, worked on dribbling skills and ball control, did lots of general exercises and finished the day with practice matches.

The school playing area was by the side of a narrow road which led to the local city office and supermarket. People would pass by and see a white-haired foreigner, whistle in his mouth, running around shouting instructions to a crowd of Japanese schoolboys. I became something of a local celebrity! People would make detours on Saturday afternoons to steal a glimpse of this unusual sight.

On hot summer afternoons parents of the football club boys would come and bring cool drinks for the coach. On freezing winter afternoons mothers plied me with hot soup. Sarah and I were invited to the sports club picnics and outings, where we met many of the parents. Once a year the school arranged a dinner for all the coaches of all sections of the sports club. There, too, I met many of the school teachers and parents. I got to know many parents in a very short time. People would stop me on the street and thank me for befriending their children.

In this way some of the suspicion, indifference and resistance towards the Christian fellowship was dispelled. A few boys, and even one or two of the parents, began to attend the fellowship at Ishiyama. Not only so, I could now visit a good number of homes as someone more than a complete stranger.

At times, when a boy was injured during the training sessions or practice matches, I would take him home and then visit later. Conversations such as the following often ensued: "Good afternoon, my name is McElligott, I am your son's football coach at the school. I am sorry your son was injured at the last training session. I trust he is all right now. Football can be a rough game. I do my best to look after the boys, but sometimes injuries are inevitable."

"Oh, please do not worry about him. He is all right now. We are so grateful for what you are doing for the children. My husband and I have been wanting to meet you. Won't you please come in and have a cup of tea with us?"

Upon entering the home we would soon be in conversation, which often led to natural and spontaneous opportunities to witness and testify. The Lord had opened up a method of witness and service which was particularly suited to me, and one which I thoroughly enjoyed.

Teaching football is certainly not a spiritual gift. But to coach young boys, some who had no interest in football at all but had been made to enter the club by overzealous parents who wanted to 'toughen them up', gave plenty of opportunity to exercise the gift of encouragement. This is what I sought to do.

Japanese society, even at primary-school level, is highly pressurised and acutely success oriented. The underachiever has a hard time, and quickly loses a sense of worth. Even in the primary school sports clubs, the majority of the coaches give almost all their time and attention to the naturally-gifted players, the stronger boys, and those likely to play in the first team. These boys soon become aware of this and look down on those who do not do so well. Many in my group were physically weak and lacked natural ability or enthusiasm. I tried to pay as much, even more attention to these boys. I tried to encourage them to give of their best. I would not allow the stronger, more-gifted players to call the weaker, less-gifted boys 'fools', or to laugh at their efforts. In the practice matches, I encouraged all the boys to bring as many players as possible into the game, by passing to and encouraging all the members of one's team. Many parents noticed these things and began to appreciate my efforts.

Serving the local children in this capacity was culturally relevant for two reasons. First it gave me a recognisable role in local society. It placed me on the inside, even if only to a limited degree.

It is important in a land like Japan, which has a Confucianist social ethic, that a religious leader should be seen to have some useful public role in a 'servant' capacity. Football coaching was such a role for me.

It was also culturally relevant because the Japanese did not really take up football seriously until 1964, when the Olympic Games were held in Tokyo. Consequently, there were still relatively few adults who had ever played the game seriously. I was 'tailor-made' for the job. I was, as the barber had said, "the man they were looking for."

Becoming the football coach for the local children enhanced the credibility of the local Christian fellowship, gave me a recognisable role in local society, presented me with the opportunity to exercise a spiritual gift, and opened the door for spontaneous personal witness. It also provided me with regular physical exercise into the bargain.

Shortly after my encounter with the barber the Lord opened another door of opportunity for me, an opportunity the likes of which I could never have planned for or contrived to create by myself.

It began in an unspectacular way. I was asked to preach a series of gospel messages at one of the fellowships in our association of churches. It was out in the countryside, some twenty miles from Ishiyama. Meetings were scheduled for Friday night, Saturday night, Sunday morning and Sunday night. I was to preach at each meeting and was looking forward to doing so.

A week or so before I was due at the church I received a telephone call from the leader of the Ladies' Fellowship there. She wanted to know if I would speak to the ladies of the church on the Sunday afternoon. As I was going to be at the church for the whole day, I agreed to take this extra meeting After I had agreed, the leader informed me that they would like me to speak on a particular subject, that of 'Bringing up Children'.

"Oh dear!" I thought to myself "what have I let myself in for?" The repercussions of that meeting have lasted ever since!

Having agreed to speak at the ladies' fellowship, I prepared a Bible study-cum-lecture on the Christian home. I included in this talk the relationship between husband and wife, and the relationship between parent and child. I illustrated the talk with poems from the Japanese literature I was studying and with many practical examples from our own family life. I concluded the talk with a short testimony of my conversion while a teenager.

About fifteen ladies attended the meeting. Some were not members of the church. They came only to this meeting having been attracted by the subject. After the talk, which lasted for about one hour, one of the ladies who was not a church member rose and requested permission to ask a question. This being granted she asked, "Pastor, would you be willimg to return to this town in two months' time to give this same talk at our annual Parents and Teachers Association lecture meeting?"

I told her that I would do so if she thought it would be helpful for the people to hear. She assured me it would be well received. She was the vice-president for the PTA for that year.

Two months later I returned to the town and made my way to the secondary school. I was shown to the headmaster's office and introduced to the staff and PTA officials. The headmaster then escorted me to the sports auditorium. The place was packed, a veritable sea of Japanese faces. I had not expected to see so many people. There were about 600 present. At the conclusion of the lecture the audience gave me a spontaneous round of applause.

*Some of the Christian students at Ishiyama with Sarah*

I enjoyed giving the lecture. I knew that in all probability a missionary had never given a lecture at the PTA meeting there before. The Japanese pastors in our fellowship were delighted that a Christian had been given such an opportunity. I came home glad for the opportunity and relieved that the lecture had gone so well. It had been a unique experience for me, one that I thought would not likely be repeated.

Imagine my surprise when, within. two weeks, I had an invitation to speak at another secondary school, a school less than ten miles from Ishiyama. A teacher at the previous school had been transferred to this school on the day after my lecture there. He discovered at his new school that a PTA lecture had been planned, but the speaker who had been booked months in advance was now unable to come. The PTA committee was at a loss. They did not know who to ask to come to speak. They knew it would be difficult to find a speaker at such short notice. The new teacher mentioned the PTA meeting at his previous school. As a result of this I was invited to speak.

It was a very hot day in August. I was met by the PTA president, and driven to the school. After exchanging greetings with the school officials and the mayor of the town, I was led to the school autitorium. I was astounded to see the crowd that had gathered. There were over 1,300 parents and teachers there. Row upon row of chairs had been set out. Every chair was full. People were sitting on the floor, too. Many used paper fans to cool themselves. For an hour and a half, apart from my voice, the only sound to be heard was the gentle movement of hundreds of hand-held fans.

This lecture, too, was well received. I was quite exhausted after the meeting because the auditorium was so hot, but soon revived in the headmaster's office which was air-conditioned. There the PTA officials and mayor thanked me for coming.

My visits to these two schools touched off an avalanche of invitations to speak to parents and teachers at secondary, primary and nursery schools. All wanted the same lecture. Every meeting was well attended.

I then received invitations to lecture at ladies' study groups, cultural study groups, Teachers' Trades Union seminars, Rotary Clubs and other churches. I was even invited to speak for ninety minutes at the Shiga County Hall to the headmasters of all the primary and secondary schools in the county. Even the County Association of the Post Office

Workers invited me to address their annual study seminar! The title they gave me to speak about was 'Personal Relationships at the Place of Work'. I also spoke in town halls, cultural centres, city offices and restaurants!

My name was placed on the register of recommended lecturers for primary and secondary schools in Shiga county. If any school could not find a suitable speaker for a PTA lecture, or school-sponsored lecture, the Department of Education at the County Hall recommended speakers from this list. Everywhere I spoke I was advertised and introduced as a Christian missionary or pastor. These lectures took me far and wide throughout Shiga county, and also into the cities of Kyoto and Osaka, as well as further south to the county of Nara where WEC had two churches.

I received letters and phone calls from isolated Christians who were encouraged that a Christian had been asked to speak at such public lectures. Some testified that they had found it so much easier to speak about Christ to their friends and relatives after the lecture had taken place. I sometimes received letters from non-Christians who wrote to tell me that their lives had been challenged.

At one school in Shiga county the school hall was not large enough to hold all who wished to attend. The reason for this was that the PTA at this particular school had come up with a novel idea. Because the lecture was easy to understand, they were keen that the students should listen to it with their parents. The school hall could not accommodate both groups together. They solved the problem by having the parents sit with their children in their classrooms and piping the lecture through closed-circuit television into each classroom. When the lecture was over each classroom was turned into a seminar led by the children's form master.

The most exciting development of this ministry was that I was eventually asked to lecture at schools in Ishiyama itself. Among them was the school where I was coaching the boys' football club.

The popularity of these lectures was very much a question of 'cultural relevancy'. At first, unknown to myself, I was 'scratching where they itched'. In retrospect, I can recognise how the principles previously related from Acts chapter two can be applied to this ministry.

First, I sought to be filled with the Holy Spirit. Even though these lectures were not preaching sessions, or even clear Bible study meetings, a Christian still needs to be filled with the Holy Spirit to be effective through them. Something of Christ was definitely conveyed to these large crowds. This has been proved to me by the response from both Christian and non- Christian.

Second, the exercise of the gift of teaching is necessary for such lectures to be requested again and again. One has to be recognised not only as having something worthwhile to say but also as having the ability even the authority to say it.

Third, the cultural relevance of this form of ministry lies in the fact that there was, and still is, a moral crisis in schools and homes in modern Japan. Japanese society, compared to most Western societies, is well ordered and nonviolent. However, in the late seventies and early eighties, considerable violence broke out in both the schools and homes of Japan. This was a national phenomenon. It received much publicity. In secondary schools in particular the violence sometimes reached crisis proportions.

Young teenagers were striking out at the two major authority symbols in their lives, parents and teachers. This outbreak of violence created a crisis of confidence in both parents and teachers. Japan had barred all religious teaching from the state school curriculum. In so doing it had 'thrown out the baby with the bath water'. It had reduced the possibility of using the education system to indoctrinate the population with Shinto concepts, but had also left the education system no basis for teaching morals and social ethics.

Added to this was the intense pressure placed upon many children to succeed academically. Among the children who could not succeed academically were many who lost a sense of self-worth and consequently reacted against the system. This reaction often took the form of physical violence against parents, teachers and even fellow students.

This is why teaching on the family and home, even by a Christian missionary, was seen as both relevant and acceptable.

I enjoyed this ministry very much. It provided me with a unique opportunity to learn more about Japan from the 'inside'. It led me into the offices of mayors, headmasters and high officials, from whom I learned a considerable amount about Japanese values and ways of thinking. It is a ministry that suits my personality; it is not a great strain for me to engage in it.

Finally, this ministry bore fruit. Through these opportunities to speak at PTA and other lectures we gained a certain credibility and respect within local society. This in turn extended to the fellowship in Ishiyama. Ladies began to attend the fellowship gatherings, having first heard of the church at these public meetings. A few even trusted Christ and were baptised. At one time I counted nine adults whose presence in the church was directly or indirectly a result of this ministry.

The Lord had opened a door of opportunity for widespread witness, through which He was encouraging scattered Christians throughout Shiga county, and through which He was building His church in Ishiyama.

Of all the opportunities I have ever had in Japan, this one in particular confirmed to me the value of continuing a systematic study of Japanese language and literature. I would never have been able to speak to such large crowds so often, or to city officials and headmasters with such freedom, if I had not continued to study Japanese even into my third term.

Coaching at the local boys' football club, and lecturing all over the county, gave our little family wide and sincere acceptance within the local community of Ishiyama. We were no longer on the outside seeking a way in. We were, to some degree, on the inside, with many opportunities to meet people and witness to them.

As the fellowship began to grow, the little shop became completely inadequate for our needs. It could no longer accommodate those who gathered. The congregation could now afford to rent more suitable premises. They began to search for such a building.

Quite quickly a little bungalow was found. It was very old and not very attractive, but it had ample parking space, was close to a bus stop, and was inexpensive to rent. It also had two little outbuildings which we could also rent. Because it was such an old building the landlord gave us permission to do what we liked with it. By knocking down a couple of inside walls we found we could seat thirty-five adults at a squeeze. The fellowship decided to rent this house. Sarah and I decided to rent the two extra, independent rooms to use as a school for the children. The car park provided them with a space for badminton, table tennis and other games.

At last the fellowship had premises which they could use as their own. This was a big step forward for them. Shortly after our move to these premises a few students and housewives were converted, and two or three Christians who had moved into Ishiyama transferred their membership in order to be part of us.

As the number of Christians grew the fellowship took on more and more of its financial responsibilities. As a result of this the young lady who was the first member of the church in Ishiyama became very busy. She took on the responsibilities of church secretary and treasurer. After the worship service she would often stay behind and attend to these tasks.

One Sunday she asked Sarah if she could bring a lunch each week and eat it at the church. Sarah told her to go ahead, and also told her that we would make a lunch, too, and join her, so that she would not have to eat alone. So for a few weeks she and the five of us shared our lunches and ate together once things had quietened down after the worship service. One after another began to join us. Soon hardly anybody was going home after the service. Even whole families brought their lunch and stayed behind.

Through this there developed a very joyful and relaxed time of fellowship every Sunday. Everyone would bring something to eat and lay it on the table, then everyone would eat what they fancied!

Someone called it 'Potluck', and the name stuck. It became an important part of our church life.

Christians talked freely with each other and shared testimony. Children played outside after lunch, while adults had impromptu Bible studies or discussions. There was always music and singing. Young people brought their guitars and formed a singing group. No one wanted to go home.

After a time some students brought their non-Christian friends to this meal, and sometimes to the worship service the following week. Some wives brought their husbands. This time of fellowship also resulted in spontaneous evangelism.

It is probably universally true that Sunday school children have a good nose for free food! Japan is no exception. The Sunday school finished at 10.00am, but rather than go home some children hovered around the church building waiting for the worship service to end and the lunch to begin. They would promptly seat themselves at the table and begin to decide among themselves what they would sample first.

Upon seeing this I gently reprimanded them. I told them that they could not stay. They were both surprised and disappointed, and insisted they were Sunday School children. I replied that I was aware of that but that the problem lay elsewhere. I explained to them that it would not be right for them to eat other people's lunches unless they contributed something themselves.

Having understood the system, they rushed off excitedly saying that they would get their mothers to make lunches for them. Very shortly they returned with their lunches and their mothers! The mothers wanted to know why the children needed lunches. We invited the mothers to join us, too. Some did so and came more than once.

Here again was a spontaneous evangelistic method that is very suited to modern Japanese culture. Japanese society is full of social obligation, and governed by a strict code of etiquette. This can be a considerable burden to the Japanese themselves. A joyful, relaxed meal in a fellowship atmosphere in which a complete stranger can take part without fear of incurring the burden of obligation is not common in Japanese society.

Many Japanese, especially younger people, long for such a place. Add to this the fact that within such an atmosphere they could talk about the problems involved in bringing up children, etcetera, and you have a situation which is very attractive to modern Japanese.

Once a month we extended this time to include games for the Sunday school children. The purpose of this was to give the Sunday school teachers an opportunity to befriend the children in a way which was not possible in a formal classroom atmosphere. Although primarily for the children, we found that some parents also attended and played together as families. The car park became a popular place for table tennis and badminton.

I even encouraged some reluctant fathers to attend by challenging them to table tennis matches. The Japanese have been world champions at table tennis in the past, and find it difficult to resist a challenge from a foreigner! My years of playing table tennis at the mission hall in Deptford and in the RAF stood me in good stead. I rarely lost a game!

After making the father work hard at the other end of the table we would sit down for a rest and a cup of green tea or orange juice. Before long the father would ask the usual question, "Why did you come to Japan?" Another natural opportunity to testify had presented itself!

Both Sarah and I had a number of English conversation classes which gave us contact with our neighbours and their children. During our second year in Ishiyama I was also asked to teach at the local university, which was only a few hundred yards from our flat. Again my study of Japanese poetry came in useful, for I taught a small group of students how to translate their own poetry into English. This approach proved quite popular, and through it I made a number of friends among the students.

It was Sarah who first had the idea of having open home for these students. Many were in digs and were very glad to have the opportunity of visiting a foreigner's home once a week for a good hot meal. We made our home available to the students every Wednesday night, if they rang before noon to say they were coming they got their evening meal, if they just turned up on the doorstep they got coffee and dessert!

Every Wednesday night we had between two and ten university students in our home. After the evening meal we sat around the low heated table and either talked, played games or watched a word game on the television. We always encouraged two Christian students, members of the fellowship, to be present, because these evenings presented many natural opportunities for testimony.

Wednesday evenings became a relaxed time of friendship and fellowship in which our children took part. They enjoyed the company of the students. Some students were introduced to the fellowship through this means. It also gave all the students an opportunity to experience first hand what family life in a Christian home is like. This was of great interest to most of them.

*Patrick preaching at WEC HQ*

It also provided Sarah and me with a moment of great personal joy. One particular Wednesday night the Christian students had been sharing their faith at the meal table. They spoke in a very natural way about the joy of forgiveness and the thrill of answered prayer, as they helped themselves to the food set before them. Our own children, who were always present at such times, listened to the conversation and also took part in it. After dinner the students played some games with the children. At around 9.00 pm we had a short time of prayer, after which the students all returned to their digs.

*PhD 1984*

With the students departed we then got Joy, Ruth and Ann ready for bed, tucked them in and began to clear up. The girls had only been in bed for about fifteen minutes when Ruth emerged from the bedroom and simply declared, 'Mummy, Daddy, I would like to be a real Christian too."

We had the joy of praying with her and pointing her to the Saviour. The Lord does wonderful things. We had travelled half way round the world to seek to lead Japanese to Christ yet there in our own living room it was the Japanese students who were instrumental in leading one of our own children to Him.

Some of the students who came to our house are now married with children of their own. One young man, whom we first met at our 'open house', was converted and later married one of the Christian students. They are now in the ministry with us among the fellowship of churches which grew out of WEC International in Japan.

Chapter Fourteen
# RELUCTANT CHOICE

After the first discouraging and fruitless year in Ishiyama it was wonderful to see the fellowship growing. One after another people were converted. We held our baptismal services on the beach at the camp site on Lake Biwa, and baptised converts in the lake. These were times of great joy.

Some who were baptised had overcome considerable pressure and opposition from their families who were committed to the Buddhist faith. Others withstood opposition from husbands and friends.

The first lady to attend the fellowship, the treasurer, gave up a secure and well-paid job in the fabrics design industry rather than compromise her testimony as a Christian. Another left Japan to study for three years at the WEC Missionary Training College in Tasmania. The many unsought for and unplanned opportunities to serve the local community and to witness within it, had made us increasingly busy. Football coaching, PTA lectures, English classes, teaching at the university, and open home, in addition to the regular worship and fellowship meetings at the church, all ate into the time available to us each week. We also carried the responsibility of leading the missionary fellowship, continuing language study, teaching our three children, and of being deputy leaders of the association of churches.

Of all our responsibilities the one single activity which consumed most of our time was the teaching of the children. As the three children grew older we needed to spend more time on preparation for lessons, setting homework and planning trips to interesting places like castles, factories, airports, docks, art galleries and museums, not to mention the zoo! The contents of the lessons became more specialised and difficult. (Neither Sarah nor I are trained teachers.)

As Joy approached her twelfth birthday and the commencement of secondary education, it became increasingly clear that without an even greater commitment of time for subjects like Maths and Science, we would not be able to continue the home-teaching method without seriously jeopardising Joy's educational development. Difficult choices were looming ahead. Decisions which could not be put off any longer needed to be made and acted upon.

We were a happy and united family. Living in another culture and teaching our own children had resulted in a closeness not experienced by many families in their own country. The last thing we wanted to do was to lose the joy and experience of being together. We had reached that time in our life as a missionary family which presents one of the most formidable challenges to long-term missionary service, the secondary education of missionary children.

We had already taken the long-term decision that our children would be educated in the English language. We wanted them to be as bi-cultural and as bilingual as possible. All three children were by now reasonably fluent in both English and Japanese, but their Japanese was the stronger language of the two. We needed, therefore, to continue Joy's education in English. Sending her to a Japanese secondary school would not result in a permanent solution. We needed to send her to an English-speaking school.

In our area of Japan there were no such schools within commuting distance. This fact narrowed our choice even further. Either she studied and boarded at an international school in Japan or she went to school in the UK. After exploring the possibilities in Japan, it became increasingly obvious that Joy would need to return to the UK to study. We discussed this with Joy and began to pray about the matter as a family. Joy was quite willing to return to the UK. She realised that she needed to go to a proper school.

Imagine how encouraged we were when, just at this time, friends wrote from England to say that they realised we had reached a difficult time in our development as a family, and that they would be willing to help in any way. We had not felt free to approach any of our friends with such a request. We truly thanked the Lord for the thoughtfulness of our friends. They were a young family themselves, with four school-age children of their own, but they were willing to care for one more. We had known this couple for over twenty years. They were dedicated Christians, and we held them in high esteem. We gladly accepted their offer of help and began to consider a school for Joy.

Our first thought was that Joy would live with our friends and attend the local secondary school but, upon reflection, we decided against this. We needed a contingency plan if, for any reason, our friends were suddenly unable to continue to cope with an extra daughter. Suppose that, through ill-health or any other circumstance, Joy became a burden to them? Would we be able to cope with the idea of being such an imposition? We decided to arrange for Joy to enter a school with boarding facilities, so that her education would not be interrupted in the event of an emergency. This meant putting Joy into a private school. It would be a considerable expense for us, a fresh step of faith.

The Lord's timing was perfect. It was just as we were considering all these things that my PTA lectures became so popular. Every time I lectured I received a fee. The amount of the fee was set by the schools themselves and tended to be uniform. In Japanese culture it is very difficult to refuse such a fee. Any refusal would be interpreted as a complaint that the fee was not sufficient, or that the lecturer was in some way dissatisfied with the arrangements. Not that I really considered refusing the fee, but sometimes it seemed embarrassingly large. Even so I was in no position to refuse. Even in 1975 the fee for one lecture was normally between £100 and £120, although I have received up to £400!

All this money was channelled towards Joy's educational expenses, and fares to and from Japan for her summer holidays. The Lord was supplying a great part of our needs through this unusual means. He had arranged for the Ministry of Education in Japan to pay for our daughter's education in Kent, England!

Everything seemed to fit together perfectly. We became increasingly sure that it was right to send Joy home to the UK. We discovered, however, that correct decisions are none the less difficult to make or live by. It was a hard thing for us to do.

We began to plan for Joy's return. We set a date for the journey and talked things over with Ruth and Ann. I had assumed that Sarah would accompany Joy to the UK while I stayed in Japan to minister at the fellowship and look after Ruth and Ann. It seemed to me that Sarah would be so much better at buying all the uniform and equipment that Joy would need. I was in for a surprise!

At lunch time one day the five of us were sitting at the table talking about Joy's impending departure, when I remarked that we would miss mother while she was away with Joy. Ruth's and Ann's response was both immediate and practical. "But, Mum! We can't live on egg and chips for three weeks, and Daddy can't cook anything else!" So I came back to the UK with Joy.

It was August. We had three weeks to buy all Joy's uniform and equipment. We had said goodbye to Sarah, Ruth and Ann at Osaka International Airport, had a good journey home and were firmly ensconced in our friends' house while they were all away on holiday. Day after day Joy and I shopped for all the necessary clothing and equipment. Shoes had to be the right shape and colour, hockey boots and a lacrosse stick were necessary. We found ourselves shopping for things we had never even seen before. Every night our first task was to sew name-tapes on to every garment we had bought that day. All this was necessary because the school insisted that Joy board for the first term at least. This, they said, would enable her to adjust to school life and English society far more quickly and smoothly.

We thoroughly enjoyed ourselves going round the shops ticking off each item as we bought it. We laughed ourselves silly at the sight of Joy in her straw boater from Harrods, an essential part of the school uniform. We were having a great time, but in the back of our minds was the inescapable fact that the day of parting was drawing nearer and nearer, and nothing could put it off.

Before the term began Joy and I visited the school. We were particularly interested in the boarding section. Joy wanted to see the room in which she would live.

We were met at the school by the headmistress, a tall silver-haired spinster with a somewhat military bearing. Beside her, Joy looked quite tiny. The school, in the town of Sevenoaks in Kent, was a mixture of old and new. The original buildings were very old, but in excellent condition and very well maintained. Modern wings had been added in two directions.

The grounds were spacious, with well kept lawns, the classrooms modern and well equipped. The facilities were excellent. They included an indoor, heated swimming pool, well equipped gymnasium, squash courts and tennis courts. However, we left the school dejected. Boarding schools in August, when all the children are on holiday, are not inspiring places. I would advise any parent taking a child to see a boarding school for the first time to go when there are children there. We were shown empty classrooms, empty dining room, empty swimming pool and empty grounds.

Without the colour, movement and noise of children, our first impression of the school was that of well-ordered lifelessness. I tried to be positive by telling Joy to imagine a pool full of noisy children, a classroom full of inquisitive students and a dining room full of hungry girls. I felt I was beginning to dispel some of the obvious gloom that had settled over Joy, and which seemed to pervade the whole place, when finally we were shown the boarding section and the room where Joy would live. Upon seeing it I became enveloped in gloom myself!

The lower-form boarding section was in the old part of the school. We approached Joy's' room through a dark, narrow corridor of wooden cubicles, the walls of which seemed to extend to the high ceiling. The corridor reminded me of some monks' cloisters I had once seen in an old abbey We were told that the cubicles were the rooms of the older students, "one girl to a room".

At the end of the corridor were some larger rooms, one of which would be home for Joy. We entered the room in which she would live. The ceiling was high, giving a sense of spaciousness. In the bare room were five iron bedsteads and five little bedside lockers. The only other piece of furniture in the room was a huge chest of drawers: five drawers, one for each child. The floor was bare, polished, wooden boards. The walls had no pictures. Over the large bay window was a sturdy iron grill. Our gloom was complete.

If there is one place on earth which cries out for the presence of children, it is a lower-form, boarding-school room during the school holidays!

Having acquired all the necessary clothing and equipment. Joy and I made our way to the school the day before the new term began, the day on which all the boarders, some 140 of them, returned to start a new school year.

An informal tea had been arranged for the parents of new boarders. It was a pleasant time of greetings and niceties in a friendly and polite atmosphere, but I found it difficult to enjoy. My mind was full of the fact that my packed suitcase was in the back of the car parked just outside in the school car park. My ticket for the journey back to Japan on that very day was in my pocket. I would have to go straight from the school to the local railway station, and from there as quickly as possible to Heathrow Airport.

The school looked so much better for the presence of children, but first impressions are not easily dispelled. Joy tended to keep quite close to my side. She was not looking forward to living in a room in which she knew no one, or being in a large school in which she was a complete stranger to both staff and students alike.

Suddenly there was so much I wanted to say to Joy but I found myself standing around, cup of tea in hand, talking about the weather to people I was never likely to ever meet again. It all seemed so unreal. Nothing could stop the clock.

Joy and I slipped away into the grounds. We found a bench under a big leafy tree. There we sat and prayed together. Joy was being very brave, but the tears began to flow. No hysterics, no frantic requests for me to stay, no last minute expressions of desire to return with me to Japan. In fact, very few words at all, just tears. Leaving Joy there was one of the hardest things I have ever done.

In the life of every parent there are certain pictures indelibly printed on the memory. Among such pictures stored away in my mind are my wife's face when she held our first child, Ruth's face when she caught her first fish, and Ann swimming for the first time in the local lake.

Clearer than any of these is the picture of Joy as I drove towards the large wrought-iron gate of the school, and on my way to the local railway station.

Framed by the stone archway that held the huge wooden doors which formed the front entrance to the old part of the school, stood the headmistress and the new boarder. The silver-haired headmistress stood tall and straight. Next to her stood Joy. She looked so tiny. With a wisdom born of frugal living I had purchased a blazer two sizes too big for her. It hung on her small frame in such a way that her hands were hardly visible. From the top of the blazer peered her tearstained face, tears still streaming down it, yet still trying to be brave. The headmistress's hand lay on Joy's shoulder, which hardly reached the headmistress's waist.

It would be almost a year before we would see Joy again.

I drove towards the local station with a heavy heart, thankful for the distracting sense of urgency given to me by the need to get to Heathrow Airport. I arrived at the local station on the outskirts of London just as a train from the city arrived. Crowds of people alighted from the train and made their way quickly to hearth and home. I boarded a deserted train going in the opposite direction. I felt sorry for myself. The picture of my daughter's tearstained face still filled my mind.

The Lord Jesus promised His disciples, *"Never will I leave you; never will I forsake you"* This promise remains true today.

For most of my Christian life I had been taught that the promises of the Bible need to be claimed if they are to be experienced. No doubt this is a general rule but Jesus is not limited by general rules. I have discovered that Jesus keeps His promises even when we do not claim them. Just as He surprised His disciples in the locked room where they hid, full of fear and doubt, so He delights to surprise us, too, even though we may not have the faith or even the will to claim the promise of His presence. His faithfulness is greater than our faith!

As I sat in the empty carriage, feeling sorry for both Joy and myself a well-known verse of Scripture came to my mind, *"For God so loved the world that he gave his one and only Son, that whoever believes in him shall not perish but have eternal life* (John 3:16).*"*

I had preached from this verse many times. I had known it all my Christian life.. I was about to understand it in a deeper way.

I began to think "If it is so hard for me to leave one daughter out of three, how much more must it have grieved the Father to send His only Son? If it causes me so much sadness to leave one daughter, because we love her and want the best for her, how infinitely more painful must it have been for the Father to send His Son, not for the Son's own good or benefit, but to be spat upon, ridiculed, rejected and crucified for the likes of you and me?"

*"God made him who had no sin to become sin for us, so that in him we might become the righteousness of God* (2 Con 5:21)."

I was beginning to understand John 3:16 with an emotional depth I had not known before. The more I pondered these things the more excited I became about them. My heart filled with a fresh knowledge of God's love for both Joy and me. So much so that in the empty carriage I began to raise my hallelujahs in praise of Him who loves us so much. The Lord was there with me. He had neither left nor forsaken me. I did not have the faith to call Him, but He was there anyway!

I arrived back in Japan the following day and soon got back into our busy programme. We later learned that Joy cried herself to sleep each night for the first week and hated the school for the first month, but once she made some friends her letters became bright and positive. She quickly settled down to life in the 'real' school.

The school proved to be the right choice for her. The staff had considerable experience with bi-cultural children, there were children there from all over the world. According to Joy, there were 'even princesses from Africa!' Some teachers gave of their personal time to help Joy overcome her initial difficulties. They showed much kindness to her and gave her much encouragement. We look back with gratitude for all they did for her.

We praised God, too, for our friends who opened up their home to Joy, and cared for her as if she were their own child. Without their help we could never have stayed in Japan. The whole experience became to us an illustration of the teamwork which is necessary among Christians in order for the ministry of Christian families overseas to be maintained long term, especially during the years in which missionary children need secondary education. It was an adventure of faith, and an expression of fellowship, on behalf of all those involved.

## Chapter Fifteen
# AS YOUR OWN POETS HAVE SAID...

I continued my study of the Japanese language as an external student of London University. My previous examination results had been surprisingly good. They presented me with the opportunity to proceed to postgraduate studies. I had long since chosen a subject to study. During my preparations for first degree examinations I had come across the poetry of one of Japan's most popular *haiku* poets. I first read a few of his poems in the prescribed classical texts, which were part of the first-degree course.

At that time I knew nothing about him, but his poetry intrigued me. It was both realistic yet humorous. It contained deep insight into the lives of ordinary people, yet combined this with a touch of sarcasm and lighthearted cynical wit. It seemed to me to have 'a touch of the Cockney' about it. I had never read anything quite like it in Japan. Consequently, I chose his life and work as a subject for a thesis. It proved to be a good choice for, according to the university, no Westerner had ever made a detailed study of Kobayashi Issa. Very little of his work had ever been translated into English. I was about to become a pioneer researcher. The professors at the university seemed very pleased.

Kobayashi Issa lived from 1763 to 1827. Although born into a farming family in one of the more remote parts of Honshu, the main island of Japan, he left home with little education, to make his fortune in the city of Edo (now Tokyo) at the age of fourteen. He never made his fortune. For most of his life, unmarried and lonely he spent his days as a travelling, vagrant poet.

*Ruth and Ann at Emmanuel Grammar School Swansea.*

At times he travelled up and down the land eking out a subsistence living as little more than a beggar. At times he donned the garb of a travelling Buddhist priest to help him in his quest for alms, and to give himself some form of protection on the open road.

When he stayed in Edo for any length of time he rented accommodation in the poorest parts of the town, or stayed in the homes of rich patrons where he did menial household chores to earn his keep.

He never gained the recognition he sought, and never achieved the title of 'master poet' which he so diligently worked for. Up until the time he married at the age of 52, he was always poor, often lonely and mostly friendless. All his life he remained utterly dedicated to his poetry.

After his death, as the extent and quality of his poetry was discovered and became widely known, his work was reappraised. He has since become known as 'The Rabbie Burns of Japan'. He is now recognised as one of the three greatest *haiku* poets in the history of the *haiku* art. He is certainly the most loved of all. Japanese primary school children learn his verses in their classrooms. Japanese adults who cannot quote a verse or two from Issa are few and far between.

For me to understand, interpret and translate his work into English meant many hours of patient study and research. Although I had studied the Japanese language for thirteen years I went back to school again. Twice a month I travelled to the nearby city of Kyoto to attend a language school at which there was a teacher who specialised in Japanese literature and pre-modern Japanese language. Having no library facilities, obtaining books was a problem, but my visits to the language school also provided me with the opportunity to scour the many secondhand bookshops in Kyoto. Being a university city, Kyoto has an abundance of specialist secondhand bookshops.

Secondhand bookshops in the ancient capital and cultural centre of the nation are like tiny time capsules. Surrounded by modern shops, gaming arcades, fashion parlours and restaurants, many of the tiny bookshops have remained unchanged for years. The bookseller, more often than not with an old pair of spectacles perched on the end of his nose, sits at an old wooden desk surrounded by piles of books which he is constantly inspecting and pricing. Sometimes the only sound in the shop is the clickety-click of the old wooden abacus he has used nearly all his life. Before him in the dim lighting stretch old wooden bookshelves extending from the floor up to the ceiling. Every inch of space is used. Piles of books lie everywhere.

To the uninitiated a secondhand bookshop in Kyoto is a scene of utter confusion, but once I had learned where to search in each shop,

I could know within a matter of seconds whether there were any books on Issa or not. The bookseller knows exactly where everything is. He is meticulous in the arrangement of his stock. Not only can he tell you where every book in the shop is, he can also tell you whether he has a certain book or not, or even if he is likely to have it in the near future! In most cases he can tell you all this without any references to catalogues and the like. All the information is in his head!

With the co-operation of some booksellers who considered me a regular customer, I began to build up my own collection of books on Issa. Booksellers would kindly put aside books which might interest me. My bookshelves became lined with books on Issa. Some were worn and tattered, dating back to the early years of this century. A few were even older. Many were written in the more difficult pre-war script. Some were copiously underlined and badly worn after many years of use, while others contained the latest scholarship concerning the poet Issa. One book contained a railway ticket thirty years old. It had been used as a bookmark. Another contained a number of summer insects, squashed flat yet perfectly preserved, as some previous reader had opened and closed the book on a summer's afternoon years ago.

Before long my bookshelves groaned under the weight of my study books. My study hours were constantly filled with two topics: the Scriptures and the life and work of Kobayashi Issa.

As my studies progressed I discovered that the two were far from mutually exclusive.

The poetry of Issa in particular, and illustrations from Japanese literature in general, began to find their way into my lectures at PTA meetings, and into my preaching of the Word of God in the churches. The Japanese have a very high regard for poetry. National newspapers run poetry competitions throughout the year. These attract thousands of entries from ordinary readers. Poetry has always been a popular pursuit in Japan. Poetry clubs abound all over the country. As a result Japanese poetic sensibility is both widespread and highly developed. Everyday speech is filled with allusions to well-known verses. The ability to quote, or cleverly misquote, a line of poetry is the basis of much Japanese humour.

This popular interest in literature in general and poetry in particular presents the missionary with a veritable treasure house of material with which to illustrate lectures and sermons, in a way which cannot fail to arouse the interest of even the most casual listener.

As I studied the Scriptures in preparation for preaching I would often recall a poem that would help me to illustrate a point and at the same time stimulate interest.

Some of the poems of Issa are obvious in their application. Even though they lose much of their charm and power through translation, this is still evident even in English.

For example, when preaching on preparedness for death:

*Chiru hana ya sude ni ore mo kudari saka.*
The blossoms fall and scatter,
I too
Am already in decline!

*Shinjitaku itase itase to sakura kana*
Get ready
Get ready to die!
Say
The cherry blossoms.

*Yo no naka wa jigoku no ue no hamami kana*
This world of ours
'Tis like viewing cherry blossoms
Over hell.

When preaching on the futility of life:
*Tsuki hana ya shijukyunen no muda aruki.*
The moon, the blossoms,
Fortynine years
Of useless walking around.

*Ware ni nite chiribeta naru ya kado no hana.*
Just like me

Hanging on the branch too long
Blossoms at the gate.

*Tsuyu chiru ya ore mo onore mo ano tori.*
The dewdrops fall
And thus it will be
For you
For me.

*Toshi toru mo wakare wakare ya shiranu tabi.*
Growing old
Is just one farewell
After another
On a journey not knowing where.

When preaching on the voice of conscience:
*Nagaki yo ya kokoro no oni  ga mi o semeru.*
The long night,
Within my heart
The stings of conscience.

I also discovered that some *haiku* verses could be used to illustrate
Scriptural truth in a quite humorous way. Such *haiku*, by a well-known
poet, immediately arouses interest on the part of the listener. Here is
one simple example:

*Hasu no hana shirami tsutsuru bakari nari.*
The lotus flower blooms
Yet here am I
Picking my lice
And flicking them away.

At first glance one may wonder what on earth such a verse may have
in common with Scripture, but it presents us with an illustration of
Romans 7:19 (Good News Bible): *"I don't do the good I want to do,*

*instead I do the evil that I do not want to do".*
When Issa wrote this poem he was sitting on the porch of a rich friend's house. Issa was on a journey. Because he was a poor man he often slept in the cheapest inns, farmers' huts or in the open fields. He picked up plenty of body lice. Having arrived at his friend's house he sat on the veranda and looked out over the beautiful garden with its ornamental pond, the surface of which was covered with beautiful lotus flowers. In the background was the rolling countryside with the mountains in the distance.

As a poet, the response this should provoke from him is a verse in praise of the beauty before him, but instead all he can think about are the lice! This can be used as an illustration of the fact that, because we are made in the image of God, we instinctively know that we should be striving to be purer, more loving, truthful and kind than we are. Yet so much of our time and attention is taken up with the nitty gritty mundane things of everyday life. We soon fret, lose our tempers, and compromise the voice of God within us.
Instead of living with a song of praise unto God who made us and loves us, we live on a low plane where there is no response to Him at all. We are surrounded by His love, His grace, and His power, all so wonderfully proved to us in Christ, and yet we live as if these wonderful things are not so.
Hence, "The lotus flower blossoms, yet here am I picking my lice!'
The use of this kind of material brings the point home and creates interest in what is to follow. Many *haiku* poems can be used to illustrate Scripture without any explanation at all.
It was thrilling to see the hand of the Lord in all these things. Indeed, all things were working together for good.
The church was growing, often through unusual and unplanned means. Joy was in England, and had adjusted to school life. Ruth and Ann were well and happy. Sarah and I, though often very very busy, were in good health and experiencing daily the Lord's help and strength.
We missed Joy very much, but she was in safe hands. After her initial term as a boarder at the school in Sevenoaks, she moved to our friends' house and commuted to school from there. Our friends even altered

their home a little by building an extra wall to divide one big bedroom into two smaller rooms so that each of the children could have a room of their own. It was somewhat of a sacrifice on behalf of the other children too. After the initial adjustments Joy began to enjoy life in England but, at this stage in her life, Japan was still home to her. Along with us, she counted the days to her summer holidays which she would spend with us in Japan.

The day came when we went back to Osaka International Airport to meet her. One year had made a big difference to her. She was now a young lady, a teenager! She strode through the automatic doors from the customs section with considerable confidence. She had changed more than we had anticipated. She even sported a rat's tail hairstyle! When the summer holidays ended, it was time to say 'Goodbye' to Joy again. After hugs and kisses she walked through passport control with the nonchalant air of someone getting on a number 47 bus in Deptford High Street rather than a fourteen-year-old getting a Jumbo jet to the otherside of the world!

After Joy had left we gave ourselves to one more year in Ishiyama. The fellowship had grown to the extent that they could now call and support a Japanese pastor. Through the fellowship of pastors with which we work, a young Japanese couple were appointed to the work at Ishiyama. The fellowship welcomed and accepted them. Six months before we were due for furlough Pastor and Mrs Matsuda came to work with us. Each week his responsibilities increased while mine decreased. When we left for furlough he and his wife assumed leadership. The fellowship at Ishiyama continued to grow.

In 'Stone Mountain' Jesus had built His church. The gates of Hades (the authority of Satan) had not prevailed. It was a joy for us to leave Ishiyama. We knew that our work was finished there.

It was time to head towards the UK once more and be together again as a complete family. Almost all the Ishiyama fellowship came to see us off at the airport. After singing and prayer we were on our way again.

## Chapter Sixteen
# THE MIRACLE HOUSE

The search for furlough housing began again This time we needed to
be even more specific. Joy was approaching GCE 0 levels. It was the
wrong time to expect her to change schools. If we were to be together
as a family again, we needed to find accommodation in or around the
town of Sevenoaks, Kent. Sevenoaks is a very popular place, a lovely
residential town within easy reach of London, yet surrounded by the
beautiful Kent countryside. Rented housing, even if available, would
be very expensive.

On a map of Kent we drew a circle around Sevenoaks to indicate the
wider area in which we hoped to find a house for one year. The circle
indicated the maximum distance we felt Joy could cope with, if she
had to commute to school each day

Our friends at the mission hall in Deptford began to explore the
possibilities, but with little success. The four of us prayed about this
need every day. We also made mention of it in our printed prayer
letter.

With less than six weeks to go before we boarded the plane home to
the UK, we still had not found a suitable place. We began to think of
caravans and tents!

With five weeks to go we received a letter from a complete stranger.
In it the writer asked if we would consider using his mother's three-
bedroom house in Sevenoaks. His mother had gone to visit a retirement
home. She liked it so much she decided to stay. Her house, fully

furnished down to bath towels and chopsticks, was waiting to be used. She was glad for a missionary family to use her house, because she had prayed for missionaries all her life. No rent would be required. We could use it for as long as we wanted!

We looked up the address on our map of Sevenoaks. It was just three minutes walk to Joy's school. She could run it in two minutes!

We were amazed, delighted and so very thankful to the Lord and His people.

We wrote to the mission hall to tell them to call off the search. We explained what had happened.

The mission hall secretary, a prudent man, wrote to us saying that they would continue the search because what we explained seemed too good to be true!

Then another amazing thing happened. The mission hall secretary was also the secretary of The Shaftesbury Society. He often visited their head office in London. While there one day shortly before we returned home for furlough, he met the Christian accountant who had come to audit the Society's books. They had lunch together and began to talk of Christian things. The mission hall secretary mentioned that a family from their fellowship in Deptford were missionaries in Japan and that they were due on furlough very soon. The accountant remarked that he had recently written to a family in Japan offering them the use of his mother's house for their furlough. The accountant was the same man who had written to us! He was able to assure the mission hall secretary that his offer was genuine. The search was immediately called off.

We then received a letter from the accountant which explained how he had heard of our needs. It, too, is an amazing story, a story which illustrates very clearly the way in which the Lord plans ahead for us. After we had been in Ishiyama for two years, we received a request for help from a young couple who were planning to come to Japan to complete research for a doctoral thesis. They needed help in finding suitable housing, and assistance in the practicalities of settling down to life in Japan. Though very busy ourselves we offered our help. The young couple lived with us for a couple of days, and then moved to one of our separate rooms at the church. After a couple of weeks there, we found suitable housing for them very close to the factory where the husband planned to do his anthropological research. We gave them as much practical help and advice as they needed. They in turn, shared with us the insights received through their studies, and encouraged us with their friendship and fellowship.

Until they came to Japan, the young couple had worshipped at a large Baptist church just outside Birmingham. The pastor of this church had, since his youth, a special burden for Japan. At one time he even had a vision of himself preaching the gospel in Japan. The young couple invited the pastor and his wife to visit Japan and stay with them for a couple of weeks. During their visit I invited the pastor to preach at the fellowship in Ishiyama, while I interpreted for him. Hence, unknown to me, his vision was fulfilled. The following day the pastor and his wife visited us for a day of fellowship. I discovered that the pastor, too, was a 'Deptford boy'. His family had lived not far from the mission hall. We became firm friends. Before they returned to the UK, the pastor asked if he could receive our prayer letter. It was sent to him regularly from that time on.

Some three years later, when he read in our prayer letter that we were searching for furlough accommodation in Sevenoaks, he recalled that a young couple in his congregation had parents living there. He asked them to write to their parents to see if they could help in any way. The parents, in turn, shared our need with the eldership of their fellowship. The accountant who offered us his mother's house was also on the eldership there.

Although a complete stranger he wrote to us soon afterwards and offered us the house. To us in Japan it was indeed miraculous!

We alighted from the plane at Heathrow and were driven straight to the house in Sevenoaks. Friends from the mission hall in Deptford had filled the cupboards and refrigerator with food. Others had prepared a meal for us. We were together as a complete family again. So began a perfect furlough. The Lord had led us to green pastures. The house was everything we could have hoped for. It had a pleasant garden at the back complete with garden shed and barbecue patio. There was plenty of room for the children to play.

There was a small garden in the front, a garage and plenty of parking space. Like most houses in Sevenoaks this one was surrounded by plenty of trees and shrubbery. We woke up each morning to the sound of birds singing. The garage was spacious enough for the large, gleaming orange-coloured Volvo saloon car which had also been given to us. Our cup was full.

*The remodelled building.*

The school in Sevenoaks had been a great help to Joy in her cultural adjustment to life in England. So much so, that we decided to trust the Lord for the means to send Ruth there, too. Ann was able to enter the local Church of England primary school for the last year of her primary education.

Very soon the children had saved up and purchased the pets they had been looking forward to for so long. Our family expanded to include a beautiful silver-grey rabbit, numerous gerbils and a few hamsters. Ruth even joined a riding club and did something she had longed to do for years. She learned how to ride a horse. After five years on the top floor of an apartment block in Ishiyama, the house in Sevenoaks was all we could ever have wished for. The Lord had all the time been 'silently planning in love' for us.

Chapter Seventeen
# A LONGER STAY THAN USUAL

As for me, I had just one task I wanted to get out of the way before I could settle down and enjoy furlough. I had brought home with me a 600-page thesis entitled, *"The Life and Work of Kobayashi Issa"*. I needed to get it printed, bound and presented to the university before I could relax and enjoy our stay in Sevenoaks.

Upon payment, the university binders soon presented me with three bound copies of the thesis, two for the university and one for myself A few weeks after the university received their volumes I received word from them that a date had been set for my viva. Professors from Oxford and London Universities would meet with me and give me an oral examination.

No one, to my knowledge, had ever translated the work of Issa into English before. His life, too, is little known in the West. I was intrigued to know how the professors would examine me.

On the appointed day I made my way once again to the School of Oriental and African Studies at London University. I was guided to a library and told to wait. All was quiet. I glanced at the rows and rows of books. Most of the titles were written in the Chinese script which was by now familiar to me. I recognised a few titles I had read in Japan. I began to feel at home. Just as I decided upon which book to take from the shelf and read, a door leading off from the libary opened and I was beckoned into a reading room.

In the small reading room, which contained only a long table and some chairs, sat the professors from Oxford and London. Before them lay the copies of my thesis. I was asked to produce my own copy and the oral examination began. The first few questions were very general, and asked in a kind and courteous manner. I answered them without any problem, but I found it difficult to concentrate.

Here I was at the very place where, years before, I had been given the aptitude test as a missionary candidate before I went to Japan. The very professor who had given me that test, and concluded that I might never really master the Japanese language, had actually been due to take part in this oral examination, but was unable to attend.

The questions became more specific. I was asked about the Buddhist influence upon certain poems, the various theories concerning the translation of medieval texts, and my opinion concerning future Japanese attitudes towards Issa and his work. One or two of my translations were queried, but I was able to satisfy the professors concerning my choice of words and conclusions.

The professor from Oxford said he had found a mistake in a poem. I had mistranslated a word. He was right. Then, with a smile, he said it was the only one he could find in the whole work, if I would correct it in my copy of the thesis he would correct it in his. With that the oral examination was over. I was told to wait outside.

I returned to the rows of books. There were a few on Issa, but I had my own copies in Japan. There were many books I would have liked to read. I drew one from the shelf and sat down to read. I had read only one page when the door opened again and I was invited back into the reading room.

The professors sat as before. They each in turn smiled politely in my direction. Then one of the professors from London University stood up, offered me his hand and congratulated me upon being the first successful doctoral candidate in Japanese at London University for many years. I suddenly wanted to tell him what the University had said after my aptitude test, but I restrained myself. In any case, they had probably been right then anyway. They had simply not reckoned on the Lord's ability to undertake for His servants!

I went home to Sevenoaks to tell Sarah the good news. In the words of the professor I could consider myself 'doctored'. On the way home

I bought an expensive-looking bottle of fizzy grape juice with which to celebrate the culmination of years of study, discipline and effort, not only on my part, but on Sarah's part too.

Before we left Japan for furlough we informed the WEC fellowship there that, in all likelihood, this would be a longer absence from the field than usual. We had reached the most critical stage in our life as a missionary family. By the end of the year all three of our daughters would be in secondary education.

It would be impossible for us to take even one of them back to Japan and teach her ourselves. We needed to be very sure that each of our children was well settled and reasonably happy in Britain before we could return to our ministry in Japan. But what would we do in Britain after our furlough year was over?

With this question in our minds we attended the WEC International Conference in Kilcreggan, Scotland, in June of 1984. The field and home base leaders of WEC from all over the world gathered for three weeks of study and fellowship. We attended as the field leaders of the work in Japan.

A new International Secretary for the whole of WEC had been appointed some months previously but a suitable deputy had not been found. This problem was high on the conference agenda. How a solution to this problem was found was recorded by the British home base leader as follows:

*"The greatest awareness of God's presence and guidance came for most of us with the election of new Deputy International Secretaries. After we had been in a pea-soup fog until the eleventh hour, God gave confidence and peace during an early morning prayer time called especially to ask for new light and clarity. It came later that day. As we met as a Co-ordinating Council, what was the tentative but if informed suggestion of one person became God's shaft of light for us all. It transpired that six in the group had had Patrick and Sarah McElligott impressed upon their hearts (some before they left their home countries), but each thought that they were the only one, and that putting another name in the hat might add to the confusion. As one after another shared, light banished the fog and peace filled our hearts. The same thing was experienced on a wider scale as we shared*

*with the whole conference. Praise the Lord!"*

Our Japanese colleagues at the conference agreed that such an appointment would be good training for our future ministry in Japan. They graciously released us to take up this ministry for three years. We became Deputy International Secretaries for WEC.

This new development meant a move from the house in Sevenoaks to Bulstrode, the British head-quarters of WEC International in Gerrards Cross. As we anticipated this move from 'our' lovely house in Sevenoaks to the huge, but very beautiful, mansion in the Buckinghamshire countryside, we were faced with yet another difficult decision.

It would mean a change of school for all three daughters. In many respects it was not a difficult time for them to change schools. Joy had just finished GCE O levels, and Ann had just finished primary school. Many children change schools at these times anyway. As for Ruth, she had not yet started the O level syllabus, so a change would not be very difficult for her. What was difficult was to try to anticipate the long-term future. If and when would we return to Japan?

No missionary family can succeed in long-term overseas ministry without deep commitment on behalf of both husband and wife.

When planning ahead it is usually the husband who takes the lead, while the wife follows. But a husband will be wise not to push ahead too far, too fast. Ample time should be given for the wife to express her feelings concerning all aspects of family/ministry tensions and decisions.

This being so, it was a tremendous encouragement to me when Sarah suggested that when we moved to Bulstrode, it would be better to put Ruth and Ann into boarding school rather than into schools local to the WEC HQ. This would enable us to see how they and we, would adjust to such a change, especially if we were to return to Japan while all three children remained in the UK.

As a result of this Joy came to live with us at the WEC HQ, and attended a local grammar school to prepare for her GCE A level examinations. Ruth and Ann went off to a small Christian school in Swansea, South Wales. A school with a real family atmosphere. It only boarded missionary children of whom there were just ten: five boys and five girls! All the other pupils were day students.

With our furlough year over, we thus commenced a period of three years' ministry alongside Stewart and Marie Dinnen, our International Secretaries, as their deputies.

Joy did her A level studies in Beaconsfield and left school with a good A level grade in Japanese, and secretarial qualifications. Upon leaving school she found excellent employment in the City as a Japanese/English bilingual secretary and became financially independent.

Ruth and Ann were developing into fine students in the school in Swansea. Guardians in Sutton Coldfield had opened their hearts and homes to them as a ministry to the Master. No obstacles now stood in our way. We could recommence our overseas ministry.

## Chapter Eighteen
# CITY PASTORATE, KYOTO

We returned to Japan in September 1987 to a fresh start in more ways than one. We had expected to return to a pioneer church-planting ministry, but it was not to be.

Six weeks before we were due to return we received a letter from the Japanese leader of the fellowship of churches in which we work. A small congregation in the city of Kyoto, the ancient capital, was keen for us to go to them in a pastoral capacity. The leadership of the fellowship of churches also agreed to this ministry for us. Would we be willing for this new beginning?

We replied that we would minister wherever the leadership felt we were most needed so, after two terms of pioneer evangelism in rural Japan, we were now to become pastors of a city church.

Our two major tasks in the first three months of our fourth term were getting our 'rusty' Japanese working well again, and spending time with the Japanese pastor at Rakusei. He would be returning to a rural pastoral ministry as soon as we were ready to move to Kyoto. These tasks accomplished, we moved to a tiny apartment near Rakusei church on the western edge of the city.

It was not until we began to set up home in Kyoto that we became more deeply aware of how much we would miss the children. As we unpacked boxes that had lain unopened for three and a half years we were constantly reminded of the life we had as a family in Ishiyama, days that would never return: a school notebook among a pile of commentaries, a stuffed toy in a box of pots and pans, a child's painting we had forgotten. We had packed in haste and were now often taken by surprise. There were simply too many reminders of the fact that there were just two of us. Never had unpacking taken so long. Never had it been so lonely.

Unable to steel our hearts and pass these items by, we found ourselves, sometimes in tears, sitting among the half-emptied boxes, hearts half a world away. Two weeks would pass before the buoyancy of spirit, so necessary for a sustained ministry in a land like Japan, was restored. Kyoto became the imperial capital of Japan in the year AD 794, when it was known as the 'City of Peace and Tranquility'. It remained the capital and cultural centre of the nation until 1868 when the Emporer moved into his new palace in Tokyo. The imperial household in Japan is steeped in Shinto and Buddhist practice and tradition. Thus Kyoto became a great religious centre, and remains so to this day. Shrines and temples abound in the city.

It is a place where, although there is no outward opposition to the gospel, the spiritual battle is very fierce, so much so that many Japanese pastors consider it one of the hardest cities in Japan in which to serve. Even now, there are more shrines and temples in Kyoto than there are people who love and worship the Lord Jesus Christ. Although one-and-a-quarter million people live in the city, the average size of a congregation is around twenty-five and there are few, if any, evangelical churches with a Sunday congregation of 150.

Minds and hearts are not receptive to the gospel here. Although outwardly Kyoto is a pleasant place to live, it is permeated by a spirit of oppressiveness. From any given point it is difficult to walk 200 yards in any direction without coming across some place or object of Shinto or Buddhist worship. One is reminded of the words in Acts 17:16, *While Paul was waiting for them in Athens, he was greatly distressed to see that the city was full of idols.*

The fellowship at Rakusei had been started by 'mistake'! The WEC fellowship was deeply committed to rural evangelism. There was no plan to start evangelistic church planting in the cities. The city was a place to visit and attend language school.

In 1968 a German missionary, Miss Gisela Wind, came to study

Japanese in Kyoto. Through personal evangelism she started a small Bible study meeting in the house where she lodged. From this small beginning she received the vision to start pioneer evangelism in the city. This she did and, with the help of other missionaries, the fellowship grew. In 1977 twenty Japanese were baptised through its witness, and joined the church. In 1979 a Japanese pastor was called, and Rakusei church became a fully self-supporting congregation. From rented premises the congregation moved to a small house that it had purchased and renovated to use as a permanent meeting place. When we arrived back in Japan, and the Japanese pastor returned to a rural ministry there was a congregation of just over thirty at Rakusei church.

It is quite unusual for a self-supporting fellowship with Japanese leadership to call a missionary as pastor. In many respects it is a step backwards, but the leadership had thought the situation through. The church would in no way lose its autonomy or financial independence. We would be treated in every respect as the previous pastor, with one exception. The pastor's support, would now be paid into a central fund and be used for pioneer evangelism elsewhere. In this way Rakusei church maintained its financial independence, integrity and self-supporting status while being pastored by a missionary couple.

After three and a half years away from Japan we commenced our new ministry with all the enthusiasm of new missionaries! It was great to be back. Language ability and freedom returned quickly, aided by the necessity to preach in Japanese at least three times a week, and often four or five.

For the previous five years numbers at Rakusei had remained constant at just over thirty. There had been consistent and faithful Biblical ministry accompanied by conversions, but this was offset by the fact that others had moved away. Discouragement had set in.

As is often the case, a change of personnel created fresh interest and enthusiasm, especially in view of the fact that the new pastor and his wife were not Japanese. Members began to bring their families and friends. The number of people joining the church began to outstrip the number who left the area for study, marriage and work.

After a year at Rakusei our first major task began to come clear. The premises were inadequate. The tiny renovated house could only seat thirty-five people with any measure of comfort. At times over forty were now attending so we started a rebuilding programme. We needed to extend the premises, but some said this would be impossible. Rakusei church is very close to an old small; imperial villa. Because of this, building regulations are very strict.

However, upon enquiry, we discovered that the restrictions had been eased. The question of rebuilding was put to the fellowship, who in turn made up a budget and pledged themselves to give the £35,000 necessary to remodel and extend the building to seat eighty-five. The work was completed in May 1989.

*Burning the Buddhist family altar*

We then entered upon a year of encouraging numerical growth. Teenage children of members were converted and baptised. Some university students began to attend. A young Christian couple from America, who had come to Japan as independent, short-term, working missionaries, also joined us and made a very enthusiastic contribution to the life and evangelism of the fellowship.

All seemed set for a period of sustained growth, but we were about to share in something of the battle that the previous pastor had struggled with. In the short space of fifteen months, fifteen of our committed members left Kyoto. Some left to find employment, others to get married, and yet others simply moved house away from Kyoto. It was quite an exodus, and in some ways a set-back to the work, but the Lord had some encouragements in store for us, too. These took the form of some remarkable conversions, and some unique opportunities for an ever-expanding, wider ministry.

Few things are more encouraging than to see people converted, especially those for whom people had virtually given up hope. Mrs K was such a person.

Her two married daughters, one single daughter, and her granddaughter were all members at Rakusei, but she had shown no interest at all in the things of Christ. Her daughter had prayed for her and witnessed to her, but she was disinterested, even cynical. She was 73 years old and asthmatic. She had to go into hospital.

I visited her there a few times. She was willing to talk and joke about life in general, but openly proclaimed that the object of her life was to enjoy herself as much as possible. Very little else interested her.

One Sunday Sarah and I were at home after a busy day of ministry at the church. Not one of the three daughters had been at worship that morning, which was quite unusual. Although we were very tired Sarah felt a burden to ring and enquire after Mrs K. The resultant telephone call set off a remarkable series of events. The married daughter who received our call was surprised to hear from us, because she was just about to call us and tell us that her mother was at home. The hospital maintenance man was waxing the floors. Her mother hated the smell of the wax so had permission to spend the night at home. She had been speaking to her, and finally old Mrs K had confessed that she was not ready to die. Would we come and speak to her?

We hurried to the house. The three daughters and the granddaughter were sitting round the dining-room table with Mrs K. The old lady began to talk. She said she knew she was a sinful person in need of salvation. She was very earnest; there was no need to persuade her to listen to the gospel. God Himself had been speaking to her. What had previously been a hardened and closed heart was now an open and receptive one. After making sure she knew why Jesus had died on the cross, and explaining how she should respond in faith and repentance, we came to that precious moment when we asked her if she would pray. To the amazement of her daughters she prayed. She confessed her sinfulness, and thanked Christ for being her Saviour. After praying, she testified to the peace she had received. We baptised her there and then in the dining room.

Even her outward appearance was different. She was a changed woman. One of her daughters exclaimed, "It's a miracle! I never really believed in miracles, but I do now!"

She really was a different person. Just over six months later she died. Her victorious funeral was yet another reminder to us all that there are none so hardened that the Lord cannot reach them. None are beyond the grace of God.

Mrs F. was a complete contrast to Mrs K. She lived in a small apartment with her husband and baby daughter, a happily-married young mother. Her husband was a professional pursuit cyclist, whose hard training and self-discipline had won her admiration and respect. She received a tract through her letter box. Having read it she telephoned us to say that she would like to attend church. She had never been to a church before, everything was new to her, but she participated enthusiastically.

People with no Biblical background often bring a complete freshness to Bible study groups. While studying the life of Elijah the small group of ladies came to 1 Kings 19:11-12: *The Lord said, "Go out and stand on the mountain in the presence of the Lord, for the Lord is about to pass by" Then a great and powerful wind tore the mountains apart and shattered the rocks before the Lord, but the Lord was not in the wind. After the wind there was an earthquake. but the Lord was not in the earthquake. After the earthquake came a fire, but the Lord was not in the fire. And after the fire came a gentle whisper".*

Sarah asked the ladies why they thought the Lord spoke in a whisper In an instant Mrs F. replied, "I suppose God had so tired Himself out with all that wind, earthquake and fire He hardly had the strength left to do anything else but speak in a whisper!"

Mrs F was converted through doing one-to-one Bible study with one of the members of the ladies fellowship. Her husband attended her baptism at the church, and from time to time attended church with her after that. She was part of the 'exodus' and moved to Hiroshima.

We were sorry to see her leave Kyoto, but happy to know that she is in fellowship with a good church there.

A Japanese pastor once said to us, "In Japan a family cannot be considered completely Christian until three generations know the Lord." This is because the influence of grandparents is still very strong in Japan. This being the case, it was a great joy to us to see the first three-generation Christian family come into being at Rakusei.

Young Mrs S. was the first in her family to attend a Christian church. Pressured by the boss's wife she attended an evangelistic meeting. There for the first time she heard the story of the prodigal son. Her sympathies lay entirely with the elder brother. After all, in good Japanese tradition he had done exactly what had been expected of him. He was hardworking, faithful and diligent. As far as she was, concerned, as a young mother with sons herself, the prodigal son was not worth thinking about.

After the birth of her third son she stopped attending church. In the meantime her husband, again through the efforts of their boss's wife, had started to attend. He became a Christian and his wife began to read the Bible again. She was shocked one day to read about herself! *I do not understand what I do. For what I want to do I do not do, but what I hate I do (Romans 7:15).*

The Holy Spirit used this verse to turn her from her own efforts and receive forgiveness and power through Jesus Christ. With her husband and three sons she was rarely absent from the worship service.

"Grandma, if you keep worshipping at that altar you will end up in hell! The real God hates that altar."

Grandma looked into three pairs of dark brown eyes full of love and concern. What grandmother could easily dismiss the sincere and forthright warning given by three winsome grandsons? Grandmother was soon attending church, was converted and baptised.

Next to be converted and baptised was the eldest grandson. It was a great joy to baptise him in Lake Biwa alongside Ruth and Ann who were visiting Japan during their school summer holidays, and wanted to be baptised at the camp site which held so many happy memories for them.

The second son became a teenager. He asked to be prepared for baptism but set a baptismal date some months ahead. Asked about the delay he replied, "I am praying that I can be baptised with my grandfather."

This would be no easy thing. The grandfather was a practising Buddhist. He maintained the family Buddhist altar, and had spent considerable time and money buying a Buddhist scroll and taking it to famous temples to get it stamped as his 'ticket to heaven'. Grandfather was a quiet, unassuming man of few words.

At the invitation of his wife and grandsons he began to attend the fellowship. After a few months I visited him in his home and was enabled to lead him to Christ. The grandson's prayers were answered. Shortly before the day of the baptism we all gathered one Sunday morning on the banks of the local river for a ceremony of great significance. The day had come when grandfather, as a public testimony to his faith in Christ, would burn the Buddhist altar and the scroll he had spent so much time and money on.

It was a real family affair. As the congregation, to the surprise of passers-by, sang hymns of praise, the elderly couple, Mrs S. and her husband, and the three grandsons, all helped to prepare the altar and the scroll for public burning. Soon it was all reduced to ashes. A three-generation Christian family was born, the first in the history of Rakusei church. Mrs S.'s own mother now attends the fellowship too.

It was through the conversion of family members on one hand, and the most unlikely people on the other, that the fellowship began to recover from the 'exodus' and grow again.

Mr O. was a self-made man. A gifted musician, he had formed his own dance band which he led with his saxophone and clarinet playing. He had no time for religion in general and no interest in his wife's Christian faith in particular.  Mr O. was in his mid-fifties when he began a battle he could not win. He had cancer.

Sarah and I first met him at his daughter's wedding. She had attended the Rakusei church with her mother from the time she was a little girl. The whole band had assembled to play at the wedding reception. Mr O. played with all his might. He knew he was losing his battle. It was the last time the band would play together.

Shortly afterwards he was in hospital. I visited him regularly, and prayed with him and for him, but there seemed to be no progress. He stubbornly rejected his wife's earnest pleading to put his faith m Christ. His self-reliance was a great barrier.

As the cancer progressed and his condition deteriorated a crisis arose. A sudden operation was necessary, and he was rushed to the operating theatre. After the operation he was a changed man. As I spoke to him in his hospital bed he began to weep. He said he was afraid. He felt a deep darkness. His wife was amazed. Never had she heard him speak like this before. Never had she heard him confess to any kind of weakness, or reveal his inner feelings.

He listened quietly to the gospel message explained through Bible verses. He was ready to pray. Tearfully he confessed his sin and his need, and put his faith in Christ. Together in the room were his wife, her brother and daughter, all Christians and all in tears. The prayers of years had been answered.

Mr O. regained some strength but was unable to leave hospital for many months. I visited him regularly to pray and read. Christian relatives would gather to sing hymns in the room from time to time. Even after he was discharged from hospital we continued this practice. His favourite hymn was *"Amazing grace! How sweet the sound."* It was always his first request.

Mr O. was baptised in his hospital room. In this way he testified to all his relatives that he was a Christian. He also made it clear, especially to his aged mother, that he wanted a Christian funeral. This was a very important step for him to take, for without it he would almost certainly have been buried in the Buddhist fashion.

When Mr O. died at fifty-seven years of age his relatives gathered around the aged mother to make the funeral arrangements. When it was made clear publicly that he had requested a Christian funeral I, as pastor of Rakusei church, was entrusted with all the services related to the funeral rites. This was a great privilege and responsibility. Mr. O.'s family had been members of the local temple for over 200 years. This would be the first Christian funeral in the family history, and the largest Christian funeral ever witnessed in the neighbourhood.

There were four separate rites performed. One for the placing of the body in the coffin, a wake, the main funeral service, and a short service at the crematorium. The first and last of these rites were private, and the second and third public. At all these services Scriptures were read, Christian prayers made, and Christian hymns sung.

At the main funeral service over 300 friends and neighbours gathered. All were given a prepared explanation of the Bible teaching concerning those who die 'in Christ'. No prayers for, or to, the dead were made, no incense burned, no Buddhist chants offered. For the majority present this was their first experience of a Christian funeral. After singing Mr. O's favourite hymns the congregation heard how he had come to put his faith in Christ. This was followed by a scriptural message giving assurance of the fact that Mr. O. was with his Master, free from pain and suffering. The whole service was relayed by loudspeaker to the many neighbours who had gathered outside to pay their last respects. It was a tremendous witness, a triumphant yet very solemn occasion.

At the crematorium the dozen or so Christians gathered in one place to sing *"What a friend we have in Jesus"* for the last time. All Mr O.'s musician friends, and even his non-Christian family members, insisted on joining us. The whole occasion was a great witness to the gospel. A chain of 200 years of temple connection had been broken. We arrived home very tired, but also very thrilled to have been entrusted with the responsibility of the funeral, and at the way the Lord had undertaken for us.

Almost all the conversions we have been privileged to see at Rakusei church were the result of family witness, one-to-one contact, or personal evangelism. This is typical of most churches in Kyoto, indeed of most of Japan. Large evangelistic campaigns do take place in huge cities like Osaka and Tokyo, but it has yet to be demonstrated that they have any great and lasting impact on the growth of local churches in places like Kyoto. Consequently, the growth of Rakusei church has been relatively slow. In the six years we have been here the membership has risen to a little over fifty. We long and pray for a greater increase, but in the meantime remain encouraged by those who do come to Christ, and continue to love, trust and follow Him as Lord and Master.

Being pastors of a Japanese church has been something of a new experience for us. Like pastors anywhere we have become deeply involved in the lives of many Japanese Christians.

*Grandson and grandfather are baptised the same day.*

Conducting weddings and funerals, though linguistically daunting tasks, gives us a tremendous opportunity to meet the wider families of Christians in the fellowship, and brings us into contact with many non-Christian relatives. There is also the need for a counselling ministry in the areas of marriage, family life, children's education, and so on.

Being pastors of a local fellowship in Japan is in many ways similar to the ministry of a pastor in the UK. The major differences are that we serve in a different cultural medium, a different spiritual atmosphere, and in the Japanese language. The need for prayer support for us and the church in Japan remains just as great.

Chapter Nineteen
# A WIDER MINISTRY

Shortly after our return to Japan in 1987 I had a telephone call from an old friend. He had been waiting patiently but had telephoned the WEC headquarters from time to time to check whether we were back in Japan or not. He was by this time retired, but he still served on a local education board in Shiga county.

When he was a primary-school headmaster I had given a PTA lecture at his school. He had never forgotten it. Now he wanted to introduce me to schools in his area. So, very soon after our return, invitations to give lectures in primary and secondary schools on family life began again.

At first these lectures were confined primarily to Shiga county, but within two years invitations began to come from schools in Kyoto, and finally from our local primary school and kindergarten in Rakusei. This resulted in new members for the church ladies' fellowship.

Since then, invitations to give these lectures have come from as far afield as Hokkaido in the far north, the Tokyo area, and Osaka and Kobe to the south of Kyoto.

Because of the restrictions placed on religious instruction in schools, these lectures are not occasions for quoting the Bible, or preaching as such, but personal testimony is quite acceptable.

Even though there are restrictions on the content of these lectures, it has been demonstrated time and time again that something of Christ and the Christian message is conveyed through them. After the lectures, when there is opportunity for personal conversation, parents ask about attending a Christian fellowship or reading the Bible. Some even write to say how they felt during the lecture.

One such letter reveals clearly the effect these lectures can have upon the non-Christian. It comes from a primary-school teacher, a Mr Kishida, and is writen in English.

*18 February 1991 At school.*
*Dear Mr McElligott,*

*I beg your pardon to write to you without permission. I am one of the school teachers at the ShinAsahi Elementary School and was one of the audience at your lecture. I wanted to express my gratitude to you after the lecture but I missed the chance.*

*Thank you very much for coming on such a cold and stormy day as last Saturday, and also for giving us such a wonderful lecture on Home Education.*

*Your lecture was very clear, understandable, attractive and convincing, as it was told through your experience. It moved us deeply. As for me, I was overwhelmed thereby. The only thing I can do is to reflect upon my way of life. I must ask myself if I am living life with such responsibility and consideration as you are. I am sorry I must say, 'No, I am not'*

*I like Haiku poetry, but I did not know the meaning before you explained the Haiku by Issa. Probably most of the audience didn't and it felt strange at being taught the meaning by a foreigner.*

*Your lecture was unique, too, because you debated Home Education from the viewpoint of the husband and wife relationship. As far as I know, no one has ever lectured on the subject of bringing up children from this point of view.*

*I was very glad to be given a clear idea of love. We often use the word, but I am afraid most of us have no dear idea of the meaning of it. Please give your lecture to more and more people in Japan. I think that without a clear idea of love, the bringing up of children and their education is nothing.*

*Please give my best regards to your wife.*
*Yours sincerely,*
*J. Kishida.*

As these lectures became more widely known, churches began to incorporate them in their evangelistic campaigns and programmes. This resulted in more invitations to minister in churches all over Japan. Evangelistic meetings in the churches would be combined with a public lecture in a local hall. One such outreach in Tokyo resulted in an added evangelistic dimension to the PTA lecture ministry in schools.

I was asked to take a series of meetings to mark the thirtieth anniversary of a local church in the city of Tokyo. These meetings included an educational lecture in a local hall. Because the hiring of the hall and the content of the meeting was the responsibility of a local church there were no restrictions on the content of the lecture. Consequently, I gave all the Biblical background to the teaching on family life and the bringing up of children.

At the time I was unaware that the chief editor of the biggest publisher of Christian books in Japan was present at all the meetings. He was a member of the local church that had arranged them. After the meetings were over he suggested that the whole series of messages be made into a book and published as quickly as possible.

Within a matter of months the book *Love Between Parents - A Key to Our Children's Future* was published. It rapidly became a popular evangelistic tool all over Japan, but more exciting to us was the fact that it provided the perfect answer to the restrictions upon clear Biblical teaching at the PTA meetings in the schools. Though there is not the freedom to preach clear, Biblical messages at the PTA meetings, there is no restriction on selling the lecturer's books once the meeting is over! Because the content of the lectures and the content of the book is so similar, many are keen to read the book at their leisure at home.

Now, after each PTA lecture, a little bookstall is set up and is soon surrounded by eager customers. On average, half the number of the people at a lecture buy the book afterwards. Through the book they learn the Biblical backgrond to the lecture.

A second book in Japanese, this time about inter-personal relationships, is also available through the same publisher. This book too, will further enhance the witness in schools. In this way a further measure of depth and meaning will be given to this widespread ministry.

All this contact with the educational world resulted in a further unique experience. It lasted only one year, but was an education in itself.

In the south of Kyoto a local education board had a problem. They needed a native English speaker with good Japanese to teach part time in two secondary schools until they could find a suitable full-time teacher. Their problem was not simply to find a teacher, but to find someone who might be able to cope with the classroom situation in their schools. Discipline was bad. They did not want a young person or a novice. Someone on the board of education suggested me for the job!

This was a unique opportunity to experience the educational world of Japan from the inside, so I went to meet the board members. They explained their predicament: they wanted someone who could teach the English curriculum from the text book but at the same time introduce some moral teaching to inspire the children, but without religious instruction! The challenge was accepted for half a day a week for one academic year.

Classroom discipline in Japanese schools is probably better than in the UK, but there are exceptions. The schools that I went to were among the exceptions! Throughout the day any male teacher without a lesson to take went on patrol to try and control the groups of children who refused to go to lessons.

There were fights between teachers and students.

Lessons were disrupted by students coming in and out of ground-floor windows to greet their friends in the classrooms. From time to time the sound of breaking glass was heard. Among those in the class-rooms there were always a few who were sound asleep. Really keen students were not in the majority. How could anyone keep the interest of forty teenagers for forty minutes in such an atmosphere?

I found a solution. First, I did not let the students know that I understood every word they were saying, or that I spoke Japanese. For the first few minutes I greeted them in slow, easy English. Then I announced that I was going to tell them my life story

I gave the first easy sentence, "I was born in London," and then suddenly translated it into fluent Japanese.

The shock was visible. "This foreigner has understood all that we have been saying about him!" From then on they were subdued.

I carried on with the story, translating each sentence into Japanese. "My name is Patrick. I am fifty-three years old. I have three brothers and two sisters. We were very poor. We had no money. Once we had to live in an orphanage. We were very happy when we got a house. The house was in a very bad place. I became a bad boy. I began to smoke. I began to drink. When I was your age I was arrested."

By this time the classroom was silent. Now I began to ask questions. 'Why do you think I was arrested?"

"Who do you think was with me when I was arrested for stealing from the shop?"

"I left school when I was sixteen years old. I was not happy. In my heart I was very sad. When I was seventeen years old a great change came to my life. I became a different person. I stopped stealing. I stopped drinking. I stopped smoking. I have been happy ever since then. I am pleased to meet you. Do you have any questions?"

Invariably the first question was, "What was the change that happened to you?"

In answer to this question, I was able to tell them that I found the love of God. In no time the forty minutes were over!

I did not see anyone come to Christ through this year in the schools, but the experience certainly helped me, as a pastor, to understand the struggles of teachers and the frustrations of students in such a situation. It was yet another way of seeing Japan from the inside and, although. a very limited evangelistic opportunity, it may yet bear fruit in the future.

In our experience, evangelism in Japan is a long-term project. Through the grace of God the sudden confrontational approach does bear fruit from time to time, but evangelism is more fruitful when it moves along avenues of personal relationships which have been established through the building up of trust and respect. This takes both time and patience. Another area of ministry which was opened up to us in Kyoto is a clear illustration of this.

Kyoto is a very accessible and popular place. Since moving here we have had an increasing number of visits from friends in the UK. We look forward to these occasions very much, for they are an opportunity to renew friendship and fellowship with many who have befriended us and given us hospitality while on furlough at home. It was during the visit of one such friend that a new area of service opened up for us in Kyoto.

This friend, on business in Japan, stayed a few days with us. During this time he treated us to a meal in a traditional Japanese restaurant at a nearby river-side beauty spot. We looked forward to a pleasant evening together over a relaxed meal. Leaving our shoes at the entrance to the restaurant, we were led to a traditional Japanese tatami room, where we sat on the floor around a low table.

Our meal arrived, carefully arranged on lacquered trays, carried by a waitress dressed in a colourful kimono. We bowed our heads, said a short grace, and prepared to enjoy our meal. As we did so a Japanese lady, a complete stranger, left her own table, knelt at the head of ours and began immediately to ply the three of us with questions!

"Are you missionaries?" (She had obviously seen us say grace.) "Do you live in Kyoto? Do you teach English?"

She was very abrupt and forthright, very unlike a Japanese lady in a public place. We were quite surprised by the directness of her approach and questions. We discovered she was on the board of the local orphanage. It was her genuine concern for the children that had compelled her to approach us.

Children from broken homes, or from domestic situations which make it necessary for them to be placed in orphanages, need all the encouragement and help they can get. This is true even in affluent Japan. Children at the local orphanage all went to local schools, but none could afford the private tuition outside school that the majority of secondary school children in Japan receive. She wanted to know if we would be willing to help the orphanage children with their English, and give them as much encouragement as we could.

We did not commit ourselves and, in deference to our guest, politely exchanged visiting cards, and promised we would think about it.

Later, as we thought and prayed about this request, the Lord brought Psalm 72:4 to our attention, *"He will save the children of the needy"*. We felt we should call the lady who had approached us in the restaurant and offer our help. As a result of this she brought the entire administrative committee of the orphanage to our flat to see us. We were invited to visit the orphanage and have a meal with the children. The Japanese name of the orphanage translates into English simply as 'Wings', the idea being that somehow the children might find comfort, and a start in life. There were fifty children there from tiny toddlers to eighteen-year-olds. As one would expect from Japan the facilities were good. The children were well fed and well clothed. We sat with them in the common dining room and had a Chinese meal. It was delicious. However, no amount of external comfort and good food could disguise the fact that many of the children were suspicious of us and kept their distance. Some seemed to reject our efforts to be friendly to them.

After discussing our own circumstances and weekly programme with the staff of Wings, we agreed to give one evening a week to the children there. For the last three years, every Thursday evening from 7.00pm until 9.00pm we have given ourselves to these children. Sarah teaches English to two classes of kindergarten and primary-school children, while I teach and play Scrabble with the older children and some staff members.

Many at Wings are not true orphans, but come from homes where, through sickness or economic difficulty parents are no longer able to care for them. Some are there for their own safety. All need that extra act of love and word of encouragement that is so important to children who are forced to live away from home and parents.

It took a little while for them to get used to us, but now we receive a welcome second to none. A few of the teenagers have visited our home, and some of the children have attended the fellowship. Strong bonds of trust have been forged between us and the staff.

As I wrote earlier in this book in Japan it is important that a religious leader performs some kind of service to the local community. In Ishiyama it was coaching the local primary-school football club. Here in Kyoto it is our weekly visit to serve the children at the Wings orphanage.

Who knows what fruit there may be from such long-term service? As one after another of the children reach the age of eighteen and are obliged to leave Wings and set out on their own, we pray that they may know that our home and our hearts are open to them at any time. Meanwhile we find ourselves enriched by the enthusiastic welcome we receive every week and the friendship of the boys and girls.

The publication of my books of lectures and sermons has resulted in an ever-widening opportunity for us to minister in Japan. Often we are both invited to minister at churches, Bible-teaching conferences, evangelistic meetings, and in Bible schools. This in turn resulted in the production of a 25-minute evangelistic video which has been aired on TV in many parts of the country, and used in many churches.

Our ministry has also led us to Korea. Every year I teach for ten days in a Korean Missionary Training Institute in Seoul, helping to train young Koreans for overseas service by teaching such topics as *Cross Cultural Church Planting, Family Life on the Mission Field, Language Study and Service in an International Missionary Society.*

During these visits it has been a tremendous privilege to help Korean missionary candidates on their way overseas, and to preach to thousands in the enormous churches in their homeland.

If I were to change the title of this book I would choose the words, 'Nothing Wasted'. It is a constant source of amazement to me that, in the economy of God, none of our experiences are meaningless. If God can bring life out of death, and 'beauty from ashes', surely He can use the painful and unwelcome experiences, even from time to time when we did not know Him, to enrich and enlarge our service for Him. He has used football and table tennis, pastimes of a 'misspent youth'. He has used even the shameful past to illustrate PTA lectures, and make them more meaningful to the listeners. The officials at the orphanage had no idea that I had ever experienced orphanage life myself, but it does help us to understand the children a little better.

We have known our times of disappointment and discouragement. There have been those who professed faith only to fall away. There have been plans that never reached fruitition. There have been mistakes we wish we had never made. But through it all nothing is wasted. We can only praise God for His wisdom and patience. It is our joy to trust and follow Him.

*How good is the God we adore,*
*Our faithful unchangeable Friend,*
*Whose love is as great as His power*
*And knows neither measure nor end.*

Chapter Twenty
# THE EXTENDED TEAM

When the first men landed on the moon one of them exclaimed, "Today we stand on the shoulders of giants" Thus he paid tribute to the countless numbers of scientists, engineers and technicians whose teamwork had made their historic journey a possibility. Only a few men set foot on the surface of the moon, but their being there was the result of a tremendous team effort. We often feel like them!

During our thirty years with CLC/WEC International as missionaries to Japan, God has graciously extended our team. As our responsibilities and needs increased so the Lord added to the team, and through them He has made our long-term service in Japan a possibility and a reality. Without their continued prayer, fellowship and co-operation it would not be possible for us to serve God in Japan today.

When I first started out as a missionary I was young and single. So was Sarah. At that time the 'team' for me was the Shaftesbury Mission Hall in Deptford, the CLC/WEC home base staff, and a few personal friends. It was all that was necessary.

As our family grew and our ministry expanded, our needs and responsibilities also increased. As our needs increased so did the size of the team. Our team still includes the Shaftesbury Mission in Deptford, the WEC home staff and the few personal friends who have supported us over the past thirty years, but as our children grew and needed to be educated in England others joined the team. Some took our children's needs upon their hearts and, through the ministry of giving, helped meet that need. Through deputation and ministry in the UK, other churches began to pray for us and help us in many different practical ways. Fees for the children's correspondence courses increased each year. Then there were large bills for boarding-school fees and fares to and from Japan, but as our team increased we were always able to meet these added expenses. When we needed them, guardians stepped forward to offer their homes to our children, and cared for them as their own.

They became a very vital part of our team even altering their homes for our children's sake.

The staff at the school in Swansea were also part of our extended team, especially the house-parents who truly loved, cared for and encouraged our two younger daughters for six years. They were truly indispensable. Our children grew into fine students under their guidance. We, and our children, have been remembered faithfully in prayer at WEC, and at church gatherings all over the British Isles. Those who attend these meetings, whether large gatherings or small, are all part of our extended team.

Without the support of all these team members our long-term missionary service in Japan would have ended years ago. Every one of them is vital. We praise and thank the Lord for each one: the individuals, the churches, the prayer meetings, the families, the staff at the school in Swansea, and all our colleagues in WEC International. We do indeed stand on the shoulders of giants.

After thirty years in Japan we are still pressing on, seeking to minister wherever we are most needed as members of a fellowship led by our Japanese brothers in Christ. The privilege has been very great.

Since we returned to Japan in 1987 our children have grown into adults. Joy is now married. Ruth finishes at university in 1995, and Ann, after a year in Africa with Operation Mobilisation, started university in 1993.

However, one of the highlights of our year remains the visits of any of our children who are able to come and see us in their summer holidays, and our visits to the UK for such occasions as weddings, university entrance, graduations, or a rare holiday all together.

The ministry, the pattern of life, our circumstances all may change, but the adventure of faith continues. Above all, He remains faithful. As missionaries and parents we dedicate this testimony to our three children themselves. They have been, and are, team members too. Their presence in Japan was vital to our ministry, and still has its effect on our ministry today. Without their courage and co-operation during the last twelve years, our time of service in Japan would have been much shorter.

The times of separation have not been easy for them or for us, but our children have perservered without complaint and have learned to trust the Master for themselves, too.

To our children we leave the words of the founder of WEC International: *'If Jesus Christ be God and died for me, then no sacrifice can be too great for me to make for Him'*

Thank you, Joy, Ruth and Ann.

Kyoto, Japan

---

WEC INTERNATIONAL

United Kingdom: Gerrards Cross, Bucks, SL9 8SZ

Also in:

Australia: 48 Woodside Avenue, Straffifleld, NSW 2135.
Canada: 37 Aberdeen Avenue, Hamilton, Ontario, L8P 2N6.
Germany: WEC, Rof Hausel 4, D-65817 Eppstein.
The Netherlands: Waalstraat 40, 8303 DR Emmeloord.
New Zealand: PO Box 27-264, Mt Roskill, Auckland 1030.
Singapore: 10 Box 185, P411es City; Singapore 9117.
South Africa:10 Box 47777, Greyville 4023.
Switzerland: Falkenstrasse 10, CR-8630, Ruti
USA: Box 1707 Port Washington, PA 19034.